The Best of *Bernie's Beat*

Volume 2: Those Who Served

Stories, Interviews and Images of American Courage

By Bernie Marvin

Published in the United States by Bernard Marvin Publishing
192 Route 10, PO Box 65, Piermont, New Hampshire 03779

Most of the work contained herein was originally published in
The Bridge Weekly, North Haverhill, New Hampshire 03774

Printed in the United States of America
978-0-578-85963-7

Work set in Times Roman
Book design by Emily Newton
Cover design by Emily Newton and Bernie Marvin
Web Design and Marketing by Monique Priestley and Bernie Marvin

Cover photo: A 2nd Division Marine keeps a sharp eye out for insurgents as he and a squad of other Marines patrol deep into the mountains of Beirut, Lebanon, during a crisis there in July 1958. Image credit: *Leatherneck Magazine*, Sgt. Bernie Marvin USMC.

Dedication

The Best of Bernie's Beat, Volume 2: Those Who Served is dedicated to sons Bernie and Spencer Marvin.

"Polly and Bernie's boys" are my best friends. Polly and I admire their chosen life's work: Bernie, a Captain of Firefighters and Spencer, a Sergeant of Police.

Thank you for your work and dedication.

In Memoriam

Colonel Donald L. Dixon
United States Marine Corps

To Sgt. Bernie Marvin USMC:

Whether on Guadalcanal in 1942 or Lebanon in 1958, Marines are first to go Into the Valley. We've both gone in and come out again. May you make it as well in the future.

My Best to you.
Donald L. Dixon
Col. USMC
27 May 1959

As inscribed in the book *Into the Valley*, written by John Hershey and illustrated by Colonel Dickson, and presented to me as a gift upon my approaching discharge from the active Marine Corps. The book describes a skirmish in the island of Guadalcanal in 1942 involving the Japanese defenders, Captain Charles Riguad, USMC, his men and war correspondent Hershey. Colonel Dickson was the publisher of *Leatherneck Magazine*. I was a combat photographer with the magazine in 1958 until July 4, 1959, my date of discharge.

Table of Contents

A Note to Readers

A year ago at this time, in an age before COVID-19, I published my first book, Volume 1 of *The Best of Bernie's Beat*. It was a thoroughly exciting venture, and not only were book sales healthy, but I had agreed to several speaking engagements to talk about my book, how it came together and what was involved to have it published in print and e-book form.

Incidentally, the subject of the title, *Bernie's Beat* is a column I write for *The Bridge Weekly* newspaper published in North Haverhill, New Hampshire. When the newspaper first started out, I assisted owner Peter Kimball with founding, editing, and publishing the paper that was first circulated in 2006.

For those first issues I wrote a local column, *Bernie's Beat*. It caught on with readers, so we decided to continue it. I have written the *Bernie's Beat* column for every issue of *The Bridge Weekly* produced since then for a total of more than 800 columns.

Publisher Peter Kimball and his wife Shauna have endured these columns over the years, and I appreciate this. It is unusual—in these times of dwindling local papers and increased political venom in the local electronic and printed media—that anyone lasts in a job that results in creating or publishing any degree of public comment.

That is why *The Bridge Weekly* took steps in the beginning to avoid the political arguments or gory junk being published in other journals scattered around the region. It seems the only time a community would get news coverage from the out of town dailies or weeklies would be for a reporter to hunt down some sordid story that interested few readers. Residents got tired of that.

Volume 1 of *The Best of Bernie's Beat* published in November 2019 included 178 pages of updated *Bernie's Beat* columns. This book you are now reading consists of interviews about military veterans that I researched, wrote, and produced for *Bernie's Beat* over a long period of time.

Some of the columns in this book are newly written and have not yet been published as a *Bernie's Beat* piece. I receive many interview suggestions from readers because they have a unique story to tell, and I am slowly getting through that list.

Self-publishing is a mystery to many unpublished writers I meet. They have a book or two inside them, but to get it from their mind and fingertips onto paper, get that paper organized and made error-free and finally see their cherished work in the form of a printed or electronic book is something way out there beyond their imagination.

I have met many good writers, photographers and artists who are entirely capable of producing excellent books. They have the experience and knowledge of their subjects, they have the training to write well and they have the discipline to sit down and get the manuscript completed.

But, as I have found over my writing career that began in 1968, publishing a book has undergone a deep metamorphosis, similar to techniques of processing photographs, computer science and film cameras. The up-to-date guidance I issued members of a Plymouth State University writing group about how to get their work published in 2007 should now be filed under "miscellaneous anachronistic fable." Most of what I told them is far away from what occurs today in the world of self-publishing.

I have received many comments from writers and photographers who have published in the past. Many tell me they would never attempt to do anything in the publishing field again. Never! They were ripped off and loaded down with books they still have kicking around their home and office. The boxes of books they received were badly prepared or poorly produced. They were embarrassed to show them around and would never sell them because their name was on the cover.

In today's publishing world, those of us who have gone the route of self-publishing through the efforts of Amazon and with our own publishing companies, like I have, are very pleasantly surprised at the ease of the program, the reasonable costs and the delightful results. To self-publish a book in today's market does not mean you are a loser or that you settled on finding a back-alley printer to do the work no other self-respecting printer or publisher would perform.

Can't find an agent? Don't worry about it. Publish the book yourself and hire a distribution company if that is what you think you need. My first volume of *The Best of Bernie's Beat* needed no agent or distribution expert, needed no one except myself, my editor, Emily Newton, who edited, made helpful suggestions and also designed the covers, plus the front and back matter and the overall tone of the book.

I established my own publishing company, Bernard Marvin Publishing, for my first book and now work through Amazon's Kindle Direct Publishing program for my mail-order program. Ordering enough author's copies of my book through Amazon provides me with ample numbers at a reasonable cost to sell locally and through my web and social media sites.

So, welcome to my second book. I have others planned and they are in the works.

Thank you for reading my newest book—I would really like your comments. They may be sent to berniemarvin@gmail.com.

Also, tune in to my website, which can be found online at https://bernardmarvinpublishing.com/. It is a new effort brought together with the assistance of designer Monique Priestley of Bradford, Vermont. The site is continually being updated to reflect new material I am writing. It has all been a delightful experience.

The world of writing and publishing is gratifying. I am able to write my regular load of stories and my *Bernie's Beat* column for *The Bridge Weekly* on a regular schedule, I have time to read books from my continuing list of interesting subjects pulled from a wide range of interests and I still meet wonderful people during my various assignments undertaken throughout the area.

The fun part of all this is in the notes, emails and letters I receive from readers who enjoy what I write. I regularly hear from friends and people unknown to me about a story or a mention that was interesting to them, thoughtful or an important part of my *Bernie's Beat* column.

I have included one here. It is a note from a long-time friend, Jeff "Doc" Brooks, whom I have known since he was in high school. A note like this means a lot to my writing world and I want readers to see and enjoy it as well.

"I am very honored to be able to call you my friend."

I was a young kid joining the New Hampshire Army National Guard back in 1978. I knew a lot of people—and idolized the few that I knew—that did what they had to for the fight before my time and during my time in the great country of the United States. Most of my friends either went to college or joined the US Navy; some did well, some were physically broken and some even mentally broken.

My thing was always to be different from everyone else and I did something different: I joined the Army. I went to boot camp and learned from the start to shut up or sound off as loud as I could.

After three weeks of getting pushed around like a puppet because the Army had some silly rule for being a certain height and I had to be a certain weight, well, I blew up and got my ass chewed by a Full Bird Colonel for being two pounds underweight.

I was sent home. I was pretty embarrassed about the whole deal. I then met up with this stout strapping person in town and watched him, as he was what I wanted to be: strong, forceful, always moving with a purpose and determination.

I knew of him because of his two children. I wanted to be what he was, see what he saw, do what he did. I was a little hesitant to talk to him, but I knew his wife well and explained what I was going through.

It wasn't but three days and this man came up to me and took me aside and talked with me like I was his child. He explained how things change and you never know what will happen in the future. I don't know if Bernie remembers that conversation or not, but I then began to change my looks, appearance and my interactions with my peers and friends.

It was three years after that I finally gained my weight and enlisted to be "all I can be." Thank you, Bernie, for taking your personal time to teach me a few things.

Now it's my turn to share my knowledge with the next generation back and the ones still here to claim there's acknowledgement for not only being The Few, The Proud, The Marines, but being a Veteran that survived the battles of war, mentally, physically and knowing we did what we had to do to survive.

I am very honored to be able to call you my friend, mentor, Brother, Veteran.

Jeffrey Doc Brooks
Combat Vet

Bernie Marvin
Bernard Marvin Publishing
Post Office Box 65
Piermont, New Hampshire 03779

February 2021

Stories Off the Starched Cuff

Pitching hay, C-Rats for the Sisters,
and thinking about Larry and Bryan

MY INITIAL HOT WEATHER TRAINING CAME NOT AT BOOT CAMP

(2018)

I have listened to many comments on how hot it is, or how sticky the humidity is, or how so many places are uncomfortable due to the heat indexes being so high. But it is nowhere near the temperatures of the Middle East, but more like those hot days I spent as a kid haying on Nate Moulton's Farm in Meredith, New Hampshire.

I keep track of weather on a continuing schedule because I am interested in it, and a knowledge of weather patterns is required for my emergency management work. I noticed at the beginning of the week and during certain daytime periods last weekend that heat indexes (those are temperatures reached when the temperature and the relative humidity are factored together) were slated to zoom as high as 105 degrees. That's pretty hot and damp.

During my lifetime, I have experienced high and uncomfortable temperatures. I remember those stifling, incredibly hot, unbearable, totally wilting temperatures of South Carolina when I was a boy fresh out of Winchester High School in Massachusetts.

I was part of a large group of New England kids who were hauled by train and bus from Boston's South Station to the deep south in early July 1955. We arrived at 2 AM on an island surrounded by stinking mudflats that watered our eyes with the searing sulfurous odors worse than any leather factory or pig farm stench we had experienced up north. As one of the boys described his introduction to Parris Island Recruit Depot, Parris Island, SC, "That place stank so bad it would knock a buzzard off a shit wagon."

The island hummed with sand fleas as big as bats. It was here that we were to spend the summer and early fall, at the infamous Marine Corps recruit training depot. It was quite a contrast to the sweet comforts of my home in Winchester, where my little photo business and local gals and pals were put aside while I ventured south and learned how to suffer like a boy on the way to becoming a man.

We all worked hard to learn how to exist in the damp heat, taking our dose of salt tablets every hour, running everywhere, and suffering the rant and rage of four drill instructors who thrived on high heat and anger.

That heat of the days and nights at Parris Island prepared me for my later adventure: a deployment as a Marine to the Middle East and parts of Africa, where those heat indices soared to 120 degrees day after day during those summer days when our units were on the move through those hostile regions.

Everyone and everything wilted; our heavy equipment, flak jackets, helmets, and personal items we carried were no exception. We each lugged three canteens of tepid American water and sun-warmed C-rations, including 100-percent melt-proof tropical chocolate bars that melted.

While we did acclimate to the heat and humidity somewhat over time, some Marines collapsed to the ground with heat stroke. I did my best to endure the high temperatures and, like the others, did my training, kept my mouth shut and thought about how easy those earlier hot summer haying days were.

As I recall those carefree days on the farm 60 years ago, I was a happy, uncaring, spoiled and well-fed civilian lad working my summer job as a common field boy on the Moulton Farm. Boss Nate thought his farm workers should bring some bearing to the job: move those hay forks faster and put some real effort into tasks, like he did when he was that age, and like his father did before him.

Old Nathan (his name when he was not present among us young hay boys) was a classic New Hampshire farmer filled with those old-fashioned ideas that people had back when he was a lad. That's what me and my fellow farm hands thought and said about his wife Ruth and their son Edwin. All three of them just did not have any sense of humor about our dislike of gathering hay into wind rows or pitching it up high and onto the old flatbed truck for hours and hours during those hot uncomfortable days in the farm fields that stretched from his farm on Quarry Road along several miles towards Center Harbor, 10 miles to the east.

That's the way it all appeared to us in our limited self-pitying view or our farming world. We were a group of lazy, wandering boys with other ideas in mind that did not include haying at any time whatsoever during the months of June, July, or August. It was just too hot. "Don't you have any inside work, Mr. Moulton?" we thought, but did not dare to ask.

Nathan, Ruth, and son Edwin had farmed all their lives and thought differently. They reminded us day after day that we "made hay while the sun shines, whether you are comfortable with that or not."

What I did notice, however, was that each year as the haying, manure spreading and milking chores faded in the west with the setting sun and I returned to high school, I came to accept my farming job with a touch more interest and pleasure each passing year. I found I liked working the fields and taking care of the animals, and I got used to the heat. I bragged about my summer job to my school friends.

By the time I entered my final farm summer with Nate Moulton, I was eager to get back to Meredith and begin doing chores, driving the hay truck and old gray Fordson tractor, scything hay away from the stone walls and enjoying a once-in-awhile afternoon touch of hard cider with Nathan down in his cool, dark earthen basement cider room.

I had finally made it in life, growing in stature around the Moulton Farm from being formerly hailed as "You there, whatever your name is" to "By, golly, you're no darned city boy anymore, Marvin." That was an honor, knowing I had conquered all those jobs I was told to do on the farm alongside Nate, Ruth, and Edwin.

I had "suffered" through the all-day-long working heat, getting along with others, keeping my mind on my field work and not thinking about fishing or catching bull frogs at Winter Pond in the back of my house in Winchester.

Most of all, though, Moulton farm owners put the fear of God in me that if I did not complete their required job assignments, I might be in some real trouble. So, no matter how difficult life got during the next summer in South Carolina and for a long time after that, my days on the Moulton Farm really shaped me into a fairly savvy kid who knew that older people with old-fashioned ideas were good to be around and listen to.

I completed boot camp, and prior to advanced infantry training we were all given a 10-day leave. I returned home, and while there decided to take a trip up to Meredith to see the Moulton family. It was a fun reunion. I enjoyed going to the barn and being among my animals again.

I did not really realize and appreciate it, but I missed the familiar sights and smells of the farm and the conversations with the Moultons I had come to appreciate. We sat down to one of Ruth Moulton's authentic farm meals, a noon dinner with farm potatoes, carrots, pork, or beef. It also included one of those meals I never did like: tripe.

"Have some tripe, Marvin."

"Oh, thank you sir, don't mind if I do!" I said as I drove my fork into a large piece of the pickled honeycombed lining of a cow's stomach. Delightful.

I often think about those summer days on the farm and how, as a kid, I learned a lot about working hard around good people who enjoyed their life and took time to teach me about growing up and preparing me for the difficult adventures ahead.

WITH NO JULY 4TH PARADE TO ATTEND, I CREATED MY OWN

(2020)

Because of the global COVID-19 pandemic, there was no annual July 4th parade marching along Woodsville's Central Street this year, passing over the green bridge and proceeding into Wells River, where the mile-long parade route ended.

As I recall my many marches in this patriotic parade, the weather was always beautiful. Enthusiastic crowds packed the route, cheering, and offering our troops and helpers cold water or Hatchland milk along the way. It was always a wonderful experience to gather with my fellow veterans and friends at either Butson's parking lot (now Shaw's) or at Walter Young's saw mill (now Walmart) and at exactly 11 AM, step off on to Central Street and get the show on the road.

For public health reasons in view of the dangerous virus, the local Woodsville–Wells River parade was called off like parades throughout the nation. This is the first time I can remember, since at least 1980 or so, that the streets were not filled with thousands of onlookers on July 4th.

So, for the Independence Day holiday, I devised my own parade this year, recalling some of the many people who assisted me and our veterans group to create, construct and get the stunning float or floats on the street headed towards Wells River. The first of many floats I was part of occurred in 1988, when we created an exact replica of the Iwo Jima flag raising during World War II. It was a wonderful pageant, complete with bronze camouflage skin paint, authentic battle uniforms and the correct weapons and equipment that were depicted in the famous photograph shot by Joe Rosenthal (whom I had met on two occasions when he was our special guest during our Marine Corps combat photographer reunions in Washington, DC).

Please join me as our vehicles, float and marching troops who beat out the sounds of freedom and independence—complete with our own drummer group led by the talented John Hobbs—as we begin our trek amidst thousands of parade viewers who shout out and applaud approval of our efforts.

We have to wait for the proper time to join in the line of march. This year's parade organizers Julius "Tuck" Tueckhardt and Charlie Smith are assigning positions, but as usual, we will just sneak into the line of march right here behind the best band in America, the Woodsville High School Marching Band led by Maestro David Heintz. We do this every year. Tuck was never pleased with me joining the parade out of his order, but the WHS band was always superb and their musical beat and cadence helped us glide down the street in step. I tell Tuck it won't ever happen again. Honest!

Getting this float and the veterans to one place at the same time is never easy. But the warriors always show up, some in uniform, some in parts of a uniform, always proud of their town and this great parade. I recall Bruce Robbins, Nancy and Bill Cowell, Mary Anne Dellinger and a host of others, like Paul Mayette, Charlie Hanson and Wayne Minnick, the VFW and the American Legion to mention a few, who began planning the July 4th parades again in about 1979 or 1980, maybe earlier.

As we head down the hill, I see Jack Graham walking the streets dressed as Uncle Sam. Also, along the parade route is that skipity hopping naughty bunny rabbit, darting here and there to everyone's delight. Sure enough, Frank Stiegler will be in that bunny suit. And then here comes Mike Thomas on another Rube Goldberg bicycle machine he invented.

We could not have done any of the creation of our floats without the help and guidance of veterans Bob Clifford and his son, Richard. The people responsible for scrounging up gear, transportation and weapons are here with us: Jay Holden, Howard Hatch, John Wolter, Ed Peterson, Spencer Marvin, Bernie Marvin III, Polly Marvin, Charles Nelson and David Johnson, Jr.

At the head of the parade there's the Haverhill selectmen's open vehicle with Rich Kinder, Ernie Towne and John Farnham. I see in the crowd on the sidelines the familiar faces of folks who helped us out with advice and guidance over the years: Grafton County Sheriff Herb Ash, Arthur Cheney, Larry Lasseigne, Doc Bailey, Bruce Newton and Bob Simblest. We have a slew of veterans with us including Larry Hart, Lawrence Hart, Russ Gover, Bruce Newton, Ryland Guay, Reverend Dwight Wright, Bob Ellsworth, Dick Waterman, Vern Dingman, Russell Page and Herb Morse. Thanks for your help, as usual. Couldn't do it without you.

We have plenty of family members to assist with the show. On the floats I see Patrick, Alex, Marissa and Veronica Marvin. Assisting with the logistics of building, moving, decorating these floats, plus offering advice from their experiences in life or in the military over the years, I see Jimmy Frezza, Bill Simpson, Alden Brown, Reggie Hunt, David Johnson, Sr., Ed Laviletta, Glenn Mitchell, Dean Rowden and Bill Fortier.

In the area of Maple, Pine and Elm streets, we see the Haverhill Police all along the way, holding back traffic, saluting the American

Veterans from a mix of combat actions march down Central Street in Woodsville, New Hampshire, in a Woodsville–Wells River July 4th parade. Seen left to right in front of the formation are Bernie Marvin (USMC), Bud Otterman (USN), Al Sponheimer (USA), Mike Blair (USMC), Russell Gover (USA) and Ed Peterson (USMC). Image credit: Marvin Family photo.

flags as they pass by. I carefully glance slightly to the left and see Chief Steve Savage, Ed Savoy, Jeff Williams, Terry Alexander and Wally George. A little further down the street, Charles Nelson—oh, look, there's Karen Nelson, too—Tom Chase, Bill Horne and Ron Fournier. Some of them are talking to Jim Walker, who has once again given the veterans a classic car to carry some of the older veterans in the parade. Harvey Walker, too, has given cars for the veterans. Thanks, fellas.

A guy feeling faint in the bright sun on Central Street. With him are Haverhill officers Alan Wright, Roy and Robin Irwin, Cecil Smith and Harvey Wayne Dickey. John Bagonzi comes over to us during a halt and we shoot the breeze. It is always good to talk to Coach. Then we see others come over to chat. "Howdy, folks," I say. Wow, it is Irv Coon, Bill Simpson, Wayne Fortier, Rusty Tattersall, Dave Moore, Earl Aremburg, Leeds Ackerman, Dick Waterman and Bob Adams. What a good good-looking group.

Near the reviewing stand, we get ready to give the judges a show of our pride in what we do when we participate in our July 4th parades. We halt, perform precision facing movements, render the military courtesy of a hand salute, another facing movement and off we go, over the bridge to Vermont.

I sneak a peek and there are George Clark, Steve Seminerio, Terry Robie, Al Sponheimer, Arnold Shields, Dean Page, Norm Provost, Herb Reardon and Bud Otterman. Also marching, I am always glad to see Barb Dunn and her Cubs and Scouts, marching with American flags—lots of American flags. Thanks, Barb!

Just over the bridge, we have more folks that have assisted and contributed their time to our success of winning prizes for what we do in these July 4th parades. I wink and give a thumbs up to Dr. Harry Rowe, Gerry Florentine, Ken and Marilyn Fuller, Everett Henson, Bill Englert, Eleanor Spiller, John Roden, George Karner, Frank O'Malley and Paul Lamott.

We have come to the end of my July 4th parade for 2020. It was a good march down Central Street, seeing many friends along the way, those who helped put together a wide array of military floats over the years that depicted our armed forces in action and at home from the Revolutionary War right through to Iraq and Afghanistan.

Many of those friends I mentioned have died, but their spirit of commitment and dedication to the cause lives on.

Thanks for marching with us and displaying your freedom, spirit, and independence. Your pride and determinations to create the best, most authentic floats for the adults and children to enjoy was perfect.

WHEN THE POWER LINES GO DOWN AND OUT, CONSIDER A MILITARY MRE MEAL

(2018)

Survival foods are surprisingly good and are similar to goodness of the MRE package. Honest!

Back in the day, survival food meant powdered milk, powdered eggs and yucky stuff out of a can, such is what we military guys endured while out in the bush hoping to find a live snake to fry on a stick. No kidding. It was called survival. It was a training course where we learned to live off the land…or starve.

At first snake sounded really bad, but after a while it sounded not so bad, and then, as the scanty food finds reduced, snake sounded real darned good. Tasted like chicken, our fearless leaders told us. These fellows who loved the wilderness and "living off the land" appeared to me to all be underweight due to lack of food. Skinny, malnourished, underfed. Not a healthy lifestyle such as we think of today. (I never told them that back then.)

When we finished the course, we were looking just like them. That was my introduction to survival food. Making do with what we could catch, capture or steal. Eventually those foods from the wild morphed into the powdered stuff or the pressed and formed lookalike foods we found in our C-rations, referred to as C-Rats.

Eventually, the C-Rats were replaced by the newest generation of military foods, known as the Meal Ready to Eat (MRE), or as they are referred to by today's military, Meals Rejected by Everyone.

My favorite use for today's MRE is as an emergency food supply, should something happen that would not allow us to be able to prepare food. I do receive inquiries from time to time about what the recommendations are relative to having a supply of foods on hand to feed families during a bad storm or electrical outage. My recommendation, usually, has always been to lay in a reasonable supply of MRE packets. They are a complete meal and nutritious. Putting the jokes aside about MRE meals being "Meals Rarely Edible" they do provide about 1,200 calories a day, are safe to use and they home-store well under moderate conditions.

Typical MRE meals and accompaniments you can purchase today include beef ravioli, Mexican chicken stew, vegetable lasagna and other beef, chicken and vegetarian entrees. MREs might also include crackers; bread slices; spreads such as jellies, cheeses or peanut butter and a line of desserts like cookies or brownies. They can be purchased in a complete one-meal, one-person packet, or you can find individual components as well.

For several years, our Piermont Emergency Management group set up emergency food displays at voting sessions and at town meeting time. And as mentioned, I do get inquiries still from folks about where to purchase MRE foods. I have always purchased my MRE supplies on the internet from a business known as Long Life Food Depot. They usually have a good supply of MRE meals, depending upon their demand due to worldwide or national storms, disasters and other reasons that families might turn to MREs for meals.

There are also freeze-dried foods available, there are high nutrition powders and other concoctions, but when the going gets tough, you might want to consider something like an MRE meal, as they are a dependable product and have been available since 1981.

However, I have some important disclaimers about all this, as well. If you have dietary concerns relative to salt or fat, I will not advise anyone to go the route of the MRE for an emergency food supply. They are very high in sodium and fat due to their original intention of them providing nourishment for members of the armed forces. I can tell you that if you are looking for that "home-cooked" meal taste or appearance, it might be best if you sought another type of food for your survival experience at home. MREs, like everything else provided for the military, provide a variety of foods, most of them fairly basic, but too many of them built around lots of spice and many with an overload of hotness.

When we were issued C-Rats, every Marine I served with always had a bottle of Tabasco stowed away in their pack and when we had a minute or two for chow, we dug deep, found our golden sauce and flavored the "C"s with this good home-food–reminding Tabasco.

Later, as the Tabasco use caught on throughout the military, Uncle Sam, through the goodness of his soul, provided a one-eighth fluid ounce of Tabasco in a little tiny glass bottle with each package of MREs. A little dab did it to mask the flavor and provide some bounce to an otherwise rather uninteresting dining out experience.

SOME MEMORIES NEVER FADE, ESPECIALLY WHEN THEY INVOLVE CATHOLIC SISTERS

(2016)

Payback is sweet, even if it takes 58 years.

That's the amount of time that has lapsed since I first came across the children's orphanage high in the hills of Lebanon in the Middle East. There, the Sisters of Charity and their 50 war-orphaned children cautiously watched as our mighty convoy of large military trucks, jeeps and armed Marines, escorted in the air by A1 Skyraider fighter planes and helicopters, as we approached their complex one very hot afternoon in July 1958.

I was with a platoon of US Marines and on combat patrol out of the city of Beirut where several thousand of us had landed four days earlier at the request of the Lebanese president. Forces from outside Lebanon had infiltrated into the country and were attempting to take it over and disrupt planned future elections.

The Sisters of Charity, garbed in their distinctive white flowing gowns and wide pointed white head covers, approached us slowly, not sure of our mission there. Our interpreters explained that we were friends and meant no harm to the sisters or the children—that they were not to worry about our presence as we were passing by.

Through our interpreters, one of the sisters asked if we had any food we might share with the children. Word was passed among our 50 troops to pass forward any C rations we had in our packs or pockets that we would like to share with the sisters and children.

We did that, and 100 cans of food—including chewing gum and tropical chocolate, hamburg patties, chopped steak and potatoes and

The high heat of Lebanon, often reaching 110 degrees or more, never slowed this patrol of 2nd Division Marines in the mountains of Beirut, Lebanon, during the action there in the summer and fall of 1958. Image credit: *Leatherneck Magazine*, Sgt. Bernie Marvin USMC.

other typical C Ration fare—were rounded up and presented to the sisters and their young charges. It was a happy time for everyone there to see the children delight in being handed these wonderful American treats that some of our Marines had no problem giving up.

Before we proceeded on our way, the children gathered close, and with the sisters they sang several French songs for us. In the middle of this torn country and for a most dangerous and difficult patrol we were on, I remember those minutes of happiness I and my fellow Marines felt as the children sang their delightful songs of thanks.

It was a time that I remember well, and those cheery voices and sweet, innocent children brought back thoughts of home to us all. Although we knew how vital our mission was to be in that war-torn country, chowing down on uninspiring menus of C Rations swigged down with limited amounts of warm Marine Corps water did bring us, from time to time, to a deep longing for our home and family, a kiss from Mom and some good chow.

Now, to the present: Last summer I was fortunate to win a raffle prize during a program sponsored by our local Cohase Chamber of Commerce. It was a large, expensive child's John Deere electric farm tractor complete with lights and horn. It was a beautiful thing, but I really had no use for it. If I was to win a farm tractor, I would have preferred it to be a real machine that could assist me around our home and acreage.

In any event, I won a child's toy ride-on tractor that I was too old to play with, and so were my grandchildren. My wife, Polly, and I figured it would be a nice thing to sell the tractor and give the proceeds to the local church charity for children. Little did we know that a youngster at the event had their eye on the tractor and was very disappointed when I won the prize and he didn't.

So, the child's parents made a good offer on the tractor and I said yes, we will accept that offer. They were pleased to know their funds would be forwarded by us to a charitable organization, although we weren't quite sure which charity at the time.

Our sweet and generous daughter-in-law, Marie, volunteers considerable time at a New Hampshire orphanage in the vicinity of where she and our son, Bernie, live in southern Maine.

A short time after I cashed in my toy tractor check, Marie had mentioned that the orphanage she volunteers at was at one time run by Sisters of Charity. It was all too familiar to me because that was the same order that I met many years earlier at the children's orphanage in Lebanon.

Excellent! We had now found our charity and they were to get the proceeds from the sale of the tractor I won at the raffle. The money was delivered to the orphanage and I was happy to later write them a note, telling them the money they received was in payment for their hospitality and songs sung by the children to me and my fellow Marines in July 1958, deep in the hills of Lebanon.

It was a donation, but it was really a payback for beautiful songs sung by sweet children, that for a moment back then, brought me home.

AS JULY 4TH APPROACHES, I GET A HANKERING TO START ANOTHER REVOLUTIONARY WAR UNIT

(2016)

People in Kingston, Massachusetts and surrounding communities enjoyed watching the Kingston Company of Continental Marines on parade. The KCCM was sharp, tough and popular!

Back in the old days, when the nation was looking forward to celebrating her 200th anniversary, our family and a group of friends got together and formed a military unit so we could celebrate the anniversary in grand style.

We decided to reactivate the old militia that used to drill on the town common in Kingston, Massachusetts, where we lived at the time. This was a group of locals who anticipated that the problems with Britain up the coastline a little bit in Boston would someday break out into a war. Sure enough, it did and on April 19, 1775. British troops marched to Lexington, then to Concord, where they were met by hundreds of militia men and families.

In a matter of hours, the 13 colonies were at war with Britain, and the rest is history. During the bicentennial in 1976 our Revolutionary War outfit was officially sanctioned as an authentic continuation of an actual militia unit by the State of Massachusetts, and we began participating in local parades and military gatherings.

It was a family affair for everyone involved, and it was a great learning experience for the kids. They learned a lot about the early history of not only the town they lived in, but their own families as well. Suddenly, their personal family history became important.

Our uniforms were all handmade from woolens that were created and spun in Kingston at a company known as Barnes Worsteds. Mr. Souther Barnes donated all the green and white wool for the uniforms. All the leather gear was handmade at a leather shop by Bob Bunce, who manufactured his own leather and created all our equipment for the 26 members of our Kingston Company of Continental Marines.

Our two boys were an important part of the unit. Bernie was a powder monkey and medical corpsman. Spencer was a banner bearer and powder monkey, and they both were dressed accordingly in colonial clothing and gear. They participated in all the parades and battles we had all over area. Their mother and my wife, Polly, sewed all of our family uniforms and marched with us in parades and ceremonies throughout Massachusetts, including the town of Concord, where the historic 1775 parade was held July 4, 1975. The parade included Revolutionary War units, including ours, from all over the country. Our unit proudly hailed from Kingston, an early town incorporated in the Bay State in 1726.

About 25 years ago when we lived in Haverhill, New Hampshire, just 3.9 miles up the road, I was telling a fellow resident of the town about our militia unit and he thought he would like to try to start up one in these parts. Plans were made to form the Northern Rangers, which was to be patterned after Major Robert Rogers Rangers, a French and Indian War unit that ranged in this area of New Hampshire and Vermont.

A meeting was held at the Parish Hall in Haverhill Corner and a fairly large crowd showed up, about 30 people including kids and parents. We had some Revolutionary War reenactors come from various states where they lived at one time before moving to our area.

The Marvin Family, formerly of Kingston, Massachusetts, as they gathered for another parade featuring the Kingston Company of Continental Marines, formed to honor the memories and feats of early Kingston and South Shore, Massachusetts, Sailors and Marines who fought in the Revolutionary War. As a shipbuilding port, Kingston saw the early construction of several ships of the upstart Massachusetts Colonial Navy. Ready for their July 4, 1976, Independence Day Parade are Polly and Bernie at the rear, with Marine Powder Monkey and Banner Carrier Spencer Marvin, and at right Private of Continental Marines Bernie Marvin III. The uniforms were handmade by Polly. Image credit: Marvin Family photo.

Although there were a couple of meetings held about the establishment of the Northern Rangers, it was too much for the intended founder and the idea was put on the shelf.

Last Saturday during the Strawberry Festival held on Haverhill Common, I passed by that busy festival on Saturday morning as I was heading north to cover the Woodsville High School graduation. I did notice a series of about six encampment tent sites and it really looked like a good set up for a Civil War group. The sight brought back a lot of good memories about early encampments and the families of reenactors we met.

One of the best-known reenactors of the French and Indian War or Revolutionary War era in these parts is Wayne Mitchell, who at one time served in several capacities at the Fort Number Four in Charlestown, New Hampshire. When I saw Wayne there several years ago, he was narrating a combat action between the local units at the fort and an invading group of Abnaki Indians. I've seen Wayne at many reenactments both on the common and at various places out of town. He has quite an inventory of proper gear for the periods of the French and Indian War and the Revolution, and he was especially sought after for his school visits and teaching children about some of our early local area history. He is an authority on that period of our national and local history.

Reenacting is a great family activity and we found that not only did we adults enjoy living the part, but the kids really took to it well and learned a lot about what it was like to live back in the old days when things were really much different from what exists here today.

STEVE WELLINGTON WAS A MAPLE SUGAR MAN

(2018)

I met him at my very first working fire as a Haverhill Corner Firefighter. He helped me put the fire out and I've liked him ever since that windy spring day.

I vividly remember the first day I met Steve Wellington. It was a windy day in early March of 1979. I was a brand-new member of the Haverhill Corner Fire Department. I was so new, I'd never had any training. I'd never been to a fire, and one spring day I thought I'd stop by the fire station to check out the equipment I would now be using.

Well, wouldn't you know it: Haverhill Corner Fire Chief, the late Vern Wiggins, came tearing into the station lot and said, "We got a brush fire, let's go." I jumped in the front seat of the lime green fire engine and off we sped—red lights spinning, the sirens wailing. I was on my way to my first fire, and shortly Steve and I would meet at the scene, he with a shovel in his hand and Vern and I manhandling an inch and one-half fire hose.

The maple sap was running furiously that day and Steve, an accomplished maple syrup maker, was in the middle of another long run of boiling and producing another great batch of his popular Jeffers Hill brand maple syrup. He also was in the middle of a large brush fire that had been touched off by embers from his sap boiling operation.

Steve helped Vern and I contain and finally extinguish the fire, and after about an hour we packed up and left the scene.

The next time I met Steve Wellington, I was also with the Haverhill Corner Fire Department, this time at the site of the newly renovated

Bedel Bridge that went down in huge windstorm on September 14, 1979.

Steve Wellington was the chairman of a group that was organized to rebuild the historic Bedel Bridge across the Connecticut River from Newbury to Haverhill. It was a very successful fundraising effort for Steve and his folks, and the bridge had been built and dedicated only three months earlier when the wind storm raced up the river, raised the structure off the abutments and dropped the entire bridge into the Connecticut River. The bridge was destroyed.

I remember Steve looking over the banking towards the river where the smashed, broken debris was piled in a twisted mess. That was all that remained of the bridge he had worked so hard to resurrect. He announced that he may organize another fundraising effort and rebuild the destroyed bridge.

He was very much affected by what he had seen that dreary morning, especially after the bridge had just been opened for foot traffic and people were dropping by to get a glimpse of the historic structure. It was a beautiful creation and he was very proud of the work his committee had done. In about 10 seconds the previous evening, it had all been destroyed.

During World War II, Steve—a 1943 graduate of Yale—joined the US Army Air Forces as a 2nd Lieutenant and meteorologist.

Steve was involved with many local projects, such as Alumni Hall and other important organizations in the region. He and his wonderful wife, Ruth Jeffers Wellington, were always good stewards of the land, the water, the wildlife and those things historic that mean so much to us all. They were both caring people and an important part of the resources that makes the Upper Connecticut River Valley the place it is today.

REMEMBERING JOHN BAGONZI; COACH, US ARMY CAPTAIN AND FRIEND

(2014)

Fly fishing with Captain Bagonzi. That's an experience I will never forget!

I thought I knew fly fishing well. That was until the day John Bagonzi took me up to the Ammonoosuc River in Lisbon and taught me a thing or two.

I had taken up fly fishing several years previously—it was something I enjoyed doing on trips to the Upper Connecticut River region in Pittsburg and from a kayak on Umbagog Lake in Erroll. Fly fishing was a learning experience of on-the-job training while hooking overhead tree limbs, wrapping roll-casted flies and lures around my head and trying to catch on to that arm and wrist technique that came with so much difficulty to this total lefty. But I caught on and pursued new and more daring casting techniques. Fly casting is not easy, but I practiced on the grass of our Route 10 home in Haverhill Corner, then later when we moved to Piermont, pulling small tufts of grass from my front lawn.

Earlier, I had gone fly fishing in the Ammonoosuc at the Woodsville Water and Light Water catchment, then down along the bank of the Connecticut River at Connecticut Street and the Green Bridge in Woodsville.

It was at that location while launching bugs and little plastic green frogs into the frothy late spring waters, that I heard the familiar greeting from a fellow walking by, John Bagonzi.

"Hi, Sarge, how are you doing?" he inquired as he had done on so many previous occasions when we met in Woodsville.

"Fine, Captain Bagonzi, how are you today?"

As always, John Bagonzi was in good spirits and cheery. John was always a delight to chat with, and although he was a true professional and amateur sports mogul, he and I spoke of other subjects, like local politics, people in the local news, military subjects and fishing.

To me, John Bagonzi deserved to be called "Captain." He had served in the US Army after a stint in the Reserve Officers Training Corps, later earning the rank of Captain. That was a long way above the rank of Sergeant I achieved in the service to the US Marine Corps. So, to me he remained "Captain Bagonzi," and to him, I remained "Sarge." These are salutations and terms of endearment of the highest respect and honor, and I felt good addressing him as a Captain and my friend.

I never had the honor of serving on one of Coach Bagonzi's high school or college teams, but I was aware of his accomplishments in his personal and professional background in both education and in sports and youth development. He was an accomplished master in all that he went after.

One size-up glance that morning from Captain Bagonzi as to my casting style, length and accuracy of casts, plus the swirling fishing line, and he knew that this lefty needed a few adjustments in windage and technique. His advice was gentle and simple, especially with the proper "snap" of forearm and wrist when wanting to launch the line out there into the water with some degree of accuracy, rather than just throwing it into the wild blue yonder and hoping for the best.

This conversation led to an invitation from Captain Bagonzi to accompany him to one of his favorite fishing spots on the

Ammonoosuc River in Lisbon. I happily agreed to do this, and the next week we traveled to the river, unpacked our gear and began to fish. His fly-fishing coaching continued throughout the morning, especially when I found difficulty in presenting my bait to a rising trout 50 feet away near the opposite riverbank. He would narrate how to load the line, watch the tip and to get your package on target without a lot of back and forth casting. He reminded me that the trout were not in the trees, they were in the water, that's where my fly presentations belong.

I was astounded at his casting accuracy and the length of his casts. That accuracy and finesse was something even the great Captain John A. Bagonzi could not get through to me. He would tell me to watch what he was doing and how he was doing it. He would narrate the entire process as he rolled through the routine smoothly and without effort. He was catching *beaucoup* fish, too!

But it was of no use for me—I was to remain forever an average fly fisherman, even under the tutelage of a great instructor and passionate advocate of excellence. Captain Bagonzi knew when a mediocre fly fisherman was in his presence.

So, thank you, Captain Bagonzi, for the extraordinary fishing trip. Knowing John Bagonzi has bragging rights attached, but having spent a morning on a river with him while he issued pearls of wisdom and technique was for me an ultimate honor.

FAR MORE THAN 3,000 VICTIMS MURDERED ON SEPTEMBER 11, 2001

(2010)

Since September 11, 2001, the death toll has continued to climb. I know this to be true.

A few years ago, I wrote a piece in *The Bridge Weekly* newspaper about a little boy who, along with our sons, Bernie and Spencer, were all part of the Kingston Company of Continental Marines. This was a reenactment group I founded in 1975 to accurately portray the early Marines.

The group included 19 uniformed and equipped men under muskets, along with families that included children, neighbors, and even pets. It was a snappy outfit, complete with home-spun woolen uniforms and authentic leather gear made right there in Kingston, Massachusetts. We held parades and ceremonies in eastern Massachusetts, as well as field days, competitions, mock battles and included the Kingston Elementary School fife and drum marching band as our music accompaniment.

One of several youngsters in our ranks was little Billy Hunt, a red-headed, freckle-faced kid with a raspy voice who was tasked by the commanding officer to assist with carrying a banner or during battle time, to be a Company Medic (Navy Corpsman) or even a Powder Monkey First Class. There is nothing this little guy could not or would not do. Along with our two sons, these three boys also carried water and equipment and assisted with food preparations and made the life of the commander and his Continental Marines a lot easier.

Little Billy Hunt's Dad, Larry Hunt, was also in the unit. He was a musket bearer, and in real life a history teacher at the local high school in Kingston, the Silver Lake Regional High School. Larry was a respected schoolteacher, a wonderful family man and a good friend.

Our family left that area and moved to New Hampshire in 1978 and I turned over the reins of the Marines to another member. Before I left, however, I promoted Larry Hunt to Corporal of Marines, shook the hands of all the Marines and we came up north to God's country. I never saw any of them again.

On September 11, 2001, Billy Hunt, by then an adult, was working in one of the towers at the World Trade Center in New York City. His business office area received a direct hit from one of the two hijacked airplanes that were driven into the towers. Billy Hunt was killed and his remains never located. He was married with children and left his parents, Larry and Diane, and a younger brother, Danny.

When I wrote that piece on little Billy Hunt on the September 11, 2001, Anniversary three or four years ago, somehow it was picked up by a news agency and ended up being published on the Massachusetts South Shore, where Larry Hunt saw it and read it. He immediately did an internet search, located my home phone number and called me in Piermont. We talked for a long time, mainly about our fond memories of Little Billy and the devastating effect his murder has had on the extended family; Billy's mom, Diane; the community and other people who knew our little friend as either a Powder Monkey First Class or as a responsible, loving adult dad, with a devoted wife, Jennifer, and their children, Emma, Hailey and Will. .

Larry cried while we spoke. He cried about the sweet memories we both had of the family events that surrounded the vivid memories of our time with the Continental Marine group. He was angry. It was a most difficult conversation, as I listened to my friend describe how the communities and people everywhere eagerly supported the William Christopher Hunt Memorial Scholarship Fund set up in their son's name.

He said although they have nothing physical remaining of their son, they do have a bench in their back yard, placed there in Billy's honor. Larry also told me that he and little Billy spoke often of his time in the Kingston Company of Continental Marines, where he worked so hard with my two sons to carry water or medical supplies to other Marines in the unit.

This week, I'm told that Larry Hunt died. His obituary noted he died peacefully at home. He was 66. I do not know how his end came, whether by illness or because of an accident. If someone asks me, I'll tell them he died of a broken heart. That's what killed him. I have no doubt.

When we spoke on the phone, he said several times to "Never forget what happened on September 11, 2001. Promise me, Bernie, you'll never forget."

For Little Billy Hunt. And now for Larry Hunt: "Never forget what happened on September 11, 2001." For them and all the others, I will never forget.

BRYAN GOULD HAD A SINCERE AND DEEP INTEREST IN OUR MILITARY.

(2020)

Our most interesting talk was at a sacred place where our veterans rest in sacred honor, at peace and forever.

Bryan Gould of Woodsville died on Friday, March 13, 2020. He was well known throughout the area for many reasons, one of them being that he owned and operated, with his wife Melissa, the Ricker Funeral Home. Both he and Melissa owned a caring and compassionate business. They both gained a reputation of being generous folks who were heavily involved in their community. They supported education, school athletics and civic organizations everywhere.

Every four years Woodsville High School students, through the Students Against Destructive Decisions, spearheaded a program that put together a mock fatal motor vehicle crash in the parking lot at the high school. The program involved many first responders and special units throughout the area, such as the Woodsville Police and Fire Departments, Woodsville Rescue Ambulance, the county attorney's office, local ministers and the Ricker Funeral Home.

It was always the somber moment of the ordeal, when Bryan and funeral home associate Tom Mayo would arrive on scene with their hearse to retrieve a "victim" from the mock crash. They would appear later during the victim's funeral that was also staged as part of the jarring anti-drunk driving program.

That was just one activity that Bryan did for the community, where, as one of the faces of Ricker Funeral Home, he participated

The late Bryan Gould of Woodsville, New Hampshire, hard at work at a Woodsville High School mock crash sponsored by the school's chapter of Students Against Destructive Decisions. Bryan assisted students with the event for many years. Image credit: *The Bridge Weekly*, Bernie Marvin.

in the most realistic fashion and it was very effective for the students to observe. It is impossible to endure a realistic program like that and not be greatly impressed, many students told me over the years that these programs have been held.

Whenever Bryan and I had a moment to chat, it usually ended up on the military side, the two of us talking about the latest war the country was involved in, local kids who joined the military and how proud he was of his son Scott's service in the US Army.

In July 2011 a friend of mine, Dr. Terrill Brown, a dentist who lived in Haverhill Corner, passed away. Dr. Terrill was a special friend because he served as a US Navy Corpsman during the Vietnam War and later served as a naval officer and retired in 2006. Navy Corpsmen serve as the medical arm to US Marines—they train with Marines, they are in combat with Marines and they wear a Marine uniform.

In honor to Dr. Brown and his long service to our country and the Marine Corps, I attended his funeral service in my Marine Corps dress blue uniform. His military interment service was to be held later that morning at the New Hampshire State Veterans Cemetery. At the conclusion of the service, Bryan Gould asked if I would accompany him and the late Dr. Brown to the cemetery. I said I would be honored to do that as I had never been to the New Hampshire State Veterans Cemetery.

At the conclusion of the graveside military service there, Bryan guided me on a tour of the cemetery, where we trooped the memorial walkways, visiting many of the military services special monuments and statuary. There was nothing he did not know about the background of the many locations we walked to, including the unique monument dedicated to the New Hampshire Marines, Navy Corpsmen and Chaplains. Most appropriate in view of Dr. Brown's service to both the US Navy and the US Marine Corps.

Brian asked me to stand at the monument, and it was there that he snapped a photograph. The photograph he took accompanies this column and has been posted ever since on my wife Polly's dresser.

I was very impressed with Bryan's knowledge of all that I saw for the hour we spent visiting the various tributes to veterans, military units and divisions that have been constructed on site at the New Hampshire Veterans Cemetery in Boscawen, about an hour and a half south of Haverhill.

So, it was no surprise at all for me to read in Bryan's obituary that he preferred that memorial contributions be made to the New Hampshire State Veterans Cemetery, PO Box 626, Concord, NH 03302-0626.

Bryan Gould, a good man that supported the Veterans Cemetery so well during his life and would continue to support it in death.

Their Time in Hell

On land, on sea and in the air

JOHN RODEN SAW THE BOMBS FALL AND SHIPS BLOW UP

(2012)

With the wave of patriotism he heard from his parents at home in Arlington Heights, Massachusetts, John Roden decided to join the US Army Air Forces on June 9, 1941, just six months prior to the opening guns of World War II on the morning of December 7.

When those opening guns began firing and bombs were falling, John had a front row seat to it all from his barracks located at Hickam Field, adjacent to the US Navy base at Pearl Harbor in the Hawaiian Islands. He was 18 years old.

John and I sat down for an interview at the Barge Inn Restaurant in Woodsville, John spoke of his service days that began with his going through the rigors of boot camp and climbing onto "a lunker of a ship," as he described it: the USS *Grant.*

While on the troopship, he ended up kipping in at the bottom of the ship, way down below the water line where it was noisy and crammed with men and equipment. The ocean trip took five days, they arrived at the Hawaiian air base in October 1941. He figured the crew was lucky because the same ship they were on ended up later on the bottom of the ocean during the later invasion of Africa. That was what he heard during a barracks scuttlebutt session, and he was relieved the ship got him across the Pacific and onto Hawaii.

They arrived at the air base situated beside Pearl Harbor and was assigned to a new barracks. His bunk and wall locker were located on the third deck of the new barracks and in the middle of that building was a large mess hall. He had a panoramic view through the large windows and could see ships of all descriptions coming in and out of Pearl Harbor. Because of all the activity, it was an interesting site to look at.

He was sent to gunnery fire school as part of his job as a fireman-gunner aboard the B-17 planes he was flying. His job was to put out fires or be a gunner aboard the huge bomber.

On a quiet Sunday morning, December 7, 1941, there was a great hangover factor in the barracks, as he and most of his squadron had traveled over to Honolulu for liberty. They all stayed out too late, but Sunday was a sleep-in morning and a quiet day of rest. Around 8 AM on that Sunday morning, John Roden and other men in the barracks were jolted when they heard a very loud explosion.

With that blast, he knew that some sailor or airman was going to be in trouble for setting off an explosion or firing off one of the big guns on a ship, probably by error. Sunday morning was no time to be doing that nonsense, John thought. Before long, another explosion blew up much of his mess hall in the building where he was sleeping. The loud-speaker system called for all personnel to get out of the barracks. He started running toward the stairwell and saw the thick smoke, and then heard a series of close-by loud explosions. He also saw a flight of Japanese planes advancing in the direction of Hickam Field and Pearl Harbor.

John and his barracks mates dashed out of the building and began running across the parade deck next to their barracks. He heard machine guns firing up at the planes, and the shrapnel from the bombs and machine-gun fire were wounding many of those around him, but they kept running, hoping to stay alive.

If they looked up 100 feet or less into the air they could see the Japanese planes passing low to the ground. The explosions were tremendous and he saw many deep bomb craters and a lot of wounded men falling everywhere; everyone was extremely nervous and attempting to do what they could to help the wounded. He jumped aboard a passing truck and he and others drove around picking up wounded soldiers and airmen.

Most of the wounded they picked up were badly hurt. After a while the assault ended and he and his mates were left with the burning buildings and destroyed airplanes the Japanese had blown up during their attack.

The group John was with took over an abandoned hangar and continued to bring the wounded and dead into the building for treatment or processing. It was difficult because many of the men did not have dog tags issued to them because prior to the attack, it was peacetime, and they felt dog tags were not needed in the time of peace.

As night advanced, John and those around him figured the Japanese were going to invade Hickam Field and the Pearl Harbor base. If the Japanese decided to invade that night, they would have been marching into in San Francisco within two months, he told me.

The next day everyone was issued the old 1903 Springfield bolt action rifles to fight off the possible Japanese invasion. They scattered men throughout the base, not wanting to concentrate the forces in one area in case the Japanese came back for another attack, but that attack never came.

Several years after the attack, John and his wife, Barbara, traveled to Pearl Harbor in 1969 for a sightseeing trip. He traveled with the New Hampshire Pearl Harbor Survivors Association and he reported they had an interesting time looking over all the familiar territory that he remembered so well. For John and others on the trip, it was a solemn time thinking about what he experienced that morning and for weeks following the December 7, 1941 attack.

After the bombing, John remained for a period at Hickam Field, and shipped to Midway Island to defend that base against a Japanese attack. At the end of his three-year enlistment, he was discharged and sent home just before the war ended in 1945.

He returned to the United States and settled in Pelham, New Hampshire and was soon appointed as a full-time police officer in Hudson. In the early 1950s he was named chief of police in Lisbon, then he was chief of the Hampton Police Department where he received national recognition for his handling of the 1965 Hampton Beach riots. He later returned to the North Country and became chief of police of the Haverhill, New Hampshire Police Department.

He left law enforcement for a few years—he and Barbara owned and operated the Pike General Store in Pike. He returned to law enforcement by accepting a job as chief of the Bartlett, New Hampshire Police Department until he retired in 1987. He also served as a bailiff to the Haverhill and Hanover District Courts, capping off a law enforcement career of more than 40 years.

He and Navy veteran George Karner of Bath were the two last surviving North Country members of the New Hampshire Pearl Harbor Survivors Association. John Roden performed many public speaking sessions with local schools and service clubs, telling audiences about his experiences at Pearl Harbor.

John died in 2013.

GEORGE KARNER SURVIVED THE DEADLY DECEMDER 7, 1941, RAID ON PEARL HARBOR

(2015)

The story he told me of his experiences that morning remains an important part of our country's history.

George Karner, former Bath selectman and longtime employee of Cottage Hospital, lived in Bath for many years before moving out of the area upon retirement. He and I knew each other through the various public events we attended. At my request, we sat down one day and chatted about his involvement in the December 7, 1941, Japanese attack on Pearl Harbor that opened World War II for the United States. George and I recorded our conversation, as I did with most veterans I spoke with about their combat experiences. Here's what he told me:

George joined the Navy in 1939 in New Jersey to get away from his home problems. He took his basic training and some advanced training aboard various Navy ships and was eventually transferred to *USS St. Louis*, a light cruiser. His job on the ship was a typical Sailor's deck duty assignment, which meant he sandblasted, painted or made things look good on the deck of that large war fighting vessel. About a week before December 7, 1941, his ship pulled into Pearl Harbor and tied up in the Navy Yard section there along with many other ships of the fleet.

The usual procedure for any Sunday morning with the fleet would be that Sailors could sleep in, but when the General Quarters alarm sounded, he figured it was just another one of those weekend drills. He jumped out of his sack, got dressed and quickly reported topside with the rest of the crew. Karner went to his battle station, which was the turret of a six-inch gun. The *St. Louis* was a heavily armed cruiser and Sailors and Marines crewed the weapons. It wasn't long before Karner figured out it was not a drill and they were under attack, and the *St. Louis* was in the middle of the action.

The antiaircraft guns Karner crewed on the ship were trussed up because they were being repaired. He was unable to go to his gun station, so his duties that morning were to throw everything overboard that could be a fire hazard. He got a ringside look at the Japanese Zero airplanes as they came in from all directions, low and fast. Other planes with torpedoes aimed them at what was Battleship Row, a place where the *St. Louis* had been tied up. The Japanese pilots who were streaming by just overhead appeared to be smiling— he could see them that well in the confusion.

Even though his ship had only half of her crew, they powered it up, untied the boat and backed into the Navy Yard channel to get away from the conflagration of all the ships that were being blown up, sunk or were burning during the attack. In the frenzy to back out of the Navy Yard and into the open sea, they followed what he remembered was the USS *Nevada*. The *Nevada* eventually beached itself in a shallow part of the channel out, but his ship kept backing out closer and closer to the open sea and further away from the attack.

The *St. Louis* did reach the open sea and turned to head towards the Japanese armada that had assembled quite a distance away. Navy officials told them to not go there, but to stay in the area and try to defend the harbor. He also noted that he had heard reports afterwards that his crew had gotten some of the guns into action and shot down an attacking Japanese plane.

The devastation of the attack was "pretty terrible. It was awful." He did not know anyone personally who was killed that morning among the more than 2,400 victims, but he did have several friends back in New Jersey that joined the various services and were killed in action through the various campaigns throughout the war.

He survived the Pearl Harbor attack and he and his ship then reported to Midway Island, where one of the first battles of the war was to begin shortly after the Pearl Harbor attack. His ship participated in that action, then left the Midway Island area and went to the Aleutian Islands in Alaska to halt the possible Japanese attack there as well.

Karner later received medical training as a Hospital Corpsman. He stayed at the Aleutian Islands for a period, but was transferred to an aircraft carrier, USS *Shipley Bay*. He remained with the *Shipley Bay* until the completion of his six-year hitch in the Navy in 1945.

Karner enjoyed his time in the Navy, except being at Pearl Harbor during the attack that morning. He was very fortunate in that he received good training for the job he was doing, and that in later life he used his medical skills with his civilian jobs, one of them being as a hospital supply employee with Shirley Cobb of Woodsville at Cottage Hospital. Together they staffed the Cottage Hospital supply room and issued all the required and requested supplies to various departments throughout the hospital for several years.

Cottage Hospital is where I first met George Karner and Shirley Cobb, while they were deep in the basement of the hospital tending to the various supply inventories. They had an important job there and were an efficient team.

Karner remained active with the Pearl Harbor Survivors Association of New Hampshire, and I remember seeing him during several speaking tours to local schools that included the Bethlehem School, the Bath Village School and the Haverhill Cooperative Middle School. I also remember that he told me he had been asked by Norwich University in Vermont to speak about his Pearl Harbor experiences there, as well.

Several years later, George Karner and his wife, Ruth, moved away to Waverly, Ohio, to be with family. He died in March 2010 at the age of 91.

An interesting part of Karner's action at Pearl Harbor on the morning of December 7, 1941, occurred as the *USS St. Louis* backed away from the furious action of the Japanese air power that morning. His ship and crew tried to flee the area and return to fight another day. Karner remembered the bombs falling on nearby Hickam Field, an air base close to Pearl Harbor that was also under attack. At Hickam Field at that moment was US Army Air Forces member John Roden, who was assisting with rescue work for the many wounded who were stationed at the base undergoing the vicious attack.

Roden told me during our interview of his recollections of the December 7, 1941, attack that he saw a ship backing out of the Pearl Harbor conflagration and heading out to sea. He remembered that it was the only ship he had seen that was moving, as the others were on fire or had been sunk.

Years later, Roden and Karner, who were two of the last living members of the New Hampshire Pearl Harbor Survivors Association, and also neighbors in adjoining towns of Bath and Haverhill, were swapping notes on their experiences about that December 7, 1941, morning, and it was discovered that the two men were close to each other during the action: Roden on land at Hickam Air Field dodging bombs and Karner aboard the nearby *USS St. Louis*, which was backing away from the air strike and preparing to go into action against the attackers that eventful morning.

Both men lived through the ordeal and many years later discovered they were within a half-mile of each other during the attack.

BUD OTTERMAN, US NAVY DIVE BOMBER PILOT

(2012)

Bud Otterman, a former Vermont legislator and attorney from West Topsham died recently. He was a mystery to most veterans in our group who marched with him in many Woodsville–Wells River July 4th parades.

Our parade group of former military service members belonged to all branches of the military. We banded together as veterans to construct floats depicting the armed forces in many tableaus from the Revolution through to the Gulf and Iraq Wars. We participated in many Woodsville–Wells River July 4th parades, and through the years we constructed some amazing pieces of history—many of them winning first and second place prizes. Our veterans enjoyed doing these activities and had great pride in their accomplishments. The thousands of parade watchers along the route also enjoyed our efforts.

Accompanying each float (or group of floats) there was always a contingent of troops who fell in, dressed to the right, and smartly covered down into properly aligned files. The contingent marched with precision down Central Street in Woodsville from the area of Newman Lumber, now Walmart, over to Wells River Village—a distance of about a mile.

One time when we assembled for one of those parades on a hot July 4th morning, just prior to the parade's 11-AM step off, I noticed a gentleman who had joined us for the first time. His appearance was a bit unusual: He was wearing what appeared to be leather headgear that looked to me like a flying helmet from out of the past.

For these parades, some of our veterans wore full uniforms, some wore their uniform jacket, some wore a military hat, but this was the first time I'd ever seen one of our veterans wearing a classic leather flying helmet, complete with goggles.

For this particular parade, I would be calling cadence to the marching unit and I was interested in this gentleman and his headgear. He introduced himself as "Bud Otterman of West Topsham, US Navy dive bomber pilot, joining your ranks, Sir."

This was how I met Bud Otterman that July 4th morning. He joined us for other parades, as well. Bud Otterman added a lot of class, spirit, and patriotism to our group, as he joined us on the line of march proudly wearing his US Naval aviator helmet.

Through years of Bud Otterman's dedicated service to his community and his state, I chatted with him on many occasions about a variety of subjects. Bud had joined the Navy in 1943 after graduating from Woodrow Wilson High School in Washington, DC. and was trained as a pilot to fly the SBD Douglas Dauntless Dive Bomber.

He was a lawyer and had an office in Bradford and served Vermont as a state's attorney in the 1950s. He was also elected to four terms in the Vermont House of Representatives and served his community in many other capacities.

We were proud to have Bud Otterman in our contingent and consider it an honor for him to have taken time from his busy schedule to appear with us during those July 4th parades.

DR. HARRY ROWE WAS A COMMUNITY DOCTOR, PARENT AND WORLD WAR II HERO

(2012)

Dr. Harry Rowe died, and his services were to be held at the Blue Mountain School gymnasium. This is an appropriate venue for those rites because I expect the service will be packed with people he knew and helped over the course of his 60 years as a general practitioner in the community.

Several years ago, Dr. Rowe told me the story of why he could never whistle. Seems at age nine he was kicked in the head by a horse while leading the animal back to the barn with his sister, Polly.

She quickly examined him, ran home, and reported that Harry was dead. She may not have been far from wrong. He spent nine days in the hospital and longer on his family couch recovering, but recover he did! He went on to graduate from Peacham Academy in 1930, and from the University of Vermont in 1936, and received his medical degree in 1943.

Dr. Rowe married Mary Whitney in 1940 and later went off to fight during World War II. He was with the 78th Infantry Division and served as the 303rd Medical Battalion Captain in the US Army. His distinguished service included being at the Bridge at Remagen as American forces were streaming into Germany from France.

Captain Rowe served in Texas, Virginia, West Virginia, England, France and Germany. He participated in the Battle of the Bulge in 1944 and was awarded the Bronze Star Medal. Somehow, he survived all that, returned home and set up a medical practice in Wells River where he served the community for 60 years as the area's family doctor. He also served the Wells River School Board for 61 years.

Dr. Rowe was an author, and in his book (*The Grass Grew Greener*, published a few years ago) he recounted some of his life's tales. He also published a series of letters in his book—letters written by him to his bride, Mary, while at the war front, and letters to him from her at the home front.

I had the pleasure and honor to read a few of the hundreds of letters this couple wrote back and forth during the war years when Dr. Rowe invited me to his Wells River home a few years ago. While there, we spent time reading some of those letters that were slated to be published in his soon-to-be-published book.

For example, on February 3, 1945, he wrote, "By the 28th of December we had opened another room and built triple-decker bunks, so we were holding about 15 patients all the time for some weeks. We discharged about 40 men back to duty with their companies. We were primarily interested in early or mild frostbite, and we carried out a bit of research and presented to the battalion a conclusion of our work."

During World War II, Mary Rowe raised the Rowes' young son, David, ran a boarding school in Burlington, Vermont, and performed with the Vermont Symphony Orchestra. Her activities as well as her loving relationship with her husband are reflected in her letters to Harry Rowe.

Harry Rowe's journey home at the end of the war is described in his book, *The Grass Grew Greener*: "On December 27, 1945, US Army Captain Harry Rowe and other returning American servicemen set sail for home on a Swedish passenger liner. After being battered by a North Atlantic storm for four days they docked in New York on January 5, 1946. 'I was so glad to be home,' he said, 'but after staring at my ceiling for 25 hours a day, I must have been green when I arrived.'"

I spoke with Dr. Rowe on many occasions about is war exploits in Europe. He was a wonderful, friendly man and I was deeply interested in his duties during those dark, cold days of the Battle of the Bulge and his entry into Germany as victory became nearer. I was interested in the European war front and had read quite a lot of the military history attached to those campaigns. We had some interesting conversations on the war as he lived it, day to day, dealing with the wounded, the rapid pace of his unit's movement and the fierce combat conditions.

Dr. Harry Rowe of Wells River, Vermont, was a long-serving physician in his community. During World War II, Captain Rowe, U.S. Army Medical Corps, endured the Battle of the Bulge and the fight at the Bridge at Remagen. Image credit: *The Bridge Weekly*, Bernie Marvin.

Several years ago, I was asked to set up a Memorial Day photo exhibit in the halls of Cottage Hospital in Woodsville, NH. I agreed to do that and requested many former military personnel at the hospital to bring in photos of themselves in uniform.

One day while I was putting up the display (that was supposed to appear for a week, but by public demand, was up for two months), Dr.

Rowe handed me two photos of his unit's action during the Rhine River crossing into Germany and on the Bridge at Remagen. I was somewhat familiar with that phase of the war and the combat action that took place as American GIs attempted to cross over the Rhine River on the Ludendorff Bridge at Remagen. His photos depicted some of the action involving is medical units, plus photos he took at the bridge. I was astounded with the quality of the photos and asked who shot them. He answered that he took the pictures.

When I asked which bridge it was, where was it located and on which river, he answered, "It was The Bridge at Remagen, the Ludendorff Bridge over the Rhine River."

So, there it was, the famous bridge, with books written on the battle and movies produced about its importance of the structure during the closing months of the war. The capture of the bridge shortened the war by several months. And there in my hands were two photos of the bridge taken by Dr. Rowe, this unassuming, quiet man whom I was proud to know and speak with about is exploits.

NAVY CORPSMAN STEVE SEMINERIO HAS MANY INTERESTING STORIES

(2020)

Steve Seminerio of Pike, New Hampshire, a Navy Corpsman attached to the 6th Marine Division during World War II, participated in the invasion of the island of Okinawa beginning Easter Sunday, April 1, 1945. It was the largest land battle prior to the end of World War II against the Japanese.

After Okinawa was secured, and after the end of World War II, Marines were taken off the island and sent to North China in November 1945, as many of the Chinese there were under occupation by the Japanese at that time. According to reports from the area, the residents were hungry, poor and in disarray and the Marines acted as a buffer between the Chinese Communists and Nationalists, trying to keep peace between the two after the Japanese were repatriated back to their home country.

According to a report written by Wesley Bush given to me during an interview with Steve Seminerio, plus my own research with reference books written by the eminent Marine Corps author, the late George B. Clark (also of Pike), the Marines gave jobs and food to many of the local people they met in China.

The Chinese Communists, however, were sabotaging rail lines and firing on Marine-guarded trains. Other encounters between the Chinese and the Marines became common activities as Marine Recon parties proceeded from Tientsin to Peiping and found 36 Chinese Communist roadblocks along the way. Marines were being continually fired upon by Chinese Communist troops. The Marines, as unwilling participants, were continually being drawn into the fight between the two Chinese factions.

Meanwhile, Marines were learning how to love steak and real luxury food and drink once again, and took advantage of eating in restaurants and enjoying their time away from the battlefields. They played sports and engaged with the Chinese residents. They met lots of girls and made friends rapidly, something Americans always do well in foreign countries they have liberated.

At leisure, Steve Seminerio and Marines of the 6th Division worked closely with the local Chinese people who were pleased to have US Marines among them. Members of the division's 22nd Marines got to know a young lad, Charlie Tsui. They especially liked this little boy who was quite different because he had wanted to go to school and he was intelligent. Unfortunately, the little boy's father and mother could not afford to give him any of the important necessities. So, the Marines adopted him and gave him the name "Charlie Two Shoes," which, I am told, sounded something like the American pronunciation of his Chinese name.

He lived in the military barracks and was taught how to become a young Marine, something which he carried with him all his life. Charlie was sent to American-staffed schools and they taught him the American way of life—they even had a small version of the US Marine uniform tailored to fit his diminutive frame. He spent more than four years with the Marines and was always happy to be among them.

When the Marines left China in 1949, they could not take Charlie back with them, but they promised him they would get him to America someday. Charlie continued with schooling and later went to college. Because of the harsh political considerations of the

Chinese government, Charlie was considered a revolutionary spy and was sentenced to house arrest. After President Nixon went to China in the 1970s, the relations with China were eased somewhat and Charlie regained his citizenship.

In April 1980, Charlie was successful in getting a letter out of China and into America where it was received by former Marines who knew him. They organized together to get Charlie to the United States, which they did after three years of work with immigration officials and political leaders.

Charlie Two Shoes arrived in America May 10, 1983, with Congressmen and Senators being bombarded with mail the next two years so that, hopefully, Charlie could stay in America. In September 1985 Attorney General Edwin Meese said Charlie Two Shoes could stay the United States indefinitely. On October 3, the rest of Charlie's family arrived in America. They lived in Ohio for a while, and then with the help of a lot of Marines they moved into Greensboro, North Carolina.

Charlie was a successful businessman who established a popular Chinese restaurant. He had purchased a new home and a new car and put his children through high school, with two later in college. Navy Corpsmen Steve Seminerio knew Charlie Two Shoes well and had his photograph taken with him, both in their green uniforms. He had not seen or heard from Charlie Two Shoes since he left China in 1945.

As Steve Seminerio tells it, in 1997 he was in the Ross Office Supply in Wells River, Vermont, making a copy of the 1945 photograph of himself and Charlie Two Shoes taken in China. While doing so, he made mention to his wife, Marilyn, of the copy being

U.S. Navy Corpsman and Methodist Minister Steve Seminerio of Pike, New Hampshire, landed with the U.S. Marines for the Easter Sunday 1945 assault on Japan's island of Okinawa. Steve is a familiar face, along with his lovely wife, Marilyn, at many events in and around the Pike region. As a popular minister, he assisted numerous churches and congregations for many years. He retired several years ago after faithful service to his communities and his country. Image credit: *The Bridge Weekly*, Bernie Marvin.

made and how good it was to see the image of little Charlie Two Shoes again. His conversation was overheard by a woman standing nearby.

She said, "I know to Charlie Two Shoes." Steve said it took him by surprise to hear her say that. He said the only Charlie Two Shoes he knew was halfway around the world in China and here is a woman to Wells River that also knows him? She said she met him in a restaurant that Charlie Two Shoes had opened in Chapel Hill, North Carolina.

Steve gave her a picture of him and Charlie Two Shoes and upon her visit to North Carolina, she handed it to Charlie. Steve said, "I received a note back from Charlie Two Shoes and in the note, he said, 'God bless you.'"

Steve said he later got another note and some souvenirs from Charlie Two Shoes. The woman said that the restaurant was doing really well, and the Marines still get a 10 percent discount there. He said it was wonderful to have someone in Wells River know Charlie

Two Shoes. Steve Seminerio said he will never get over it and that it "is a small world after all."

Steve Seminerio was born in Everett, Massachusetts. His family included two sisters, Anne and Helen, and he lost a brother, John, to spinal meningitis when he was 18 years old. Steve told me during an interview that his mother wanted him to "become a doctor because doctors made a lot of money and they were very prestigious." His folks were immigrants and they thought it was the ultimate thing to be wealthy like most doctors.

"My mother, Santina (Little Saint), and father, Andrew Seminerio, came to America from Sicily just before the US entered World War I in about 1916," he said. His father was a tailor and Steve was always the best dressed kid in his rough neighborhood because he had custom-made clothes sewn by his dad. His mother was a hard worker and was employed in a clothing factory. They both had nothing when they came here to America, and Steve said they had to work awfully hard to get ahead.

"That's the American way," Steve said.

Steve graduated from Boston English High School in 1943. Soon after, he started Boston University summer and fall classes. Steve enrolled in five science classes at Boston University and did not do well in any of them. It was too much of a big load, so on his 18th birthday on January 31, he enlisted in the US Navy. The Navy recruiter asked what he had done with his life so far and he said that he was a premed student at Boston University. The recruiter assigned him to the hospital corps. He attended boot camp in Sampson, New York. It was a naval training station, and when he completed boot camp in 1944, they assigned him to the Sampson Naval Hospital right there on the base.

While there, Steve received medical training as a Corpsman, and one day on the bulletin board his name appeared and announced that he was going to be serving with the Marine Corps. said he had no idea what was going to be like, so he shed his Navy gear, sent it home and put on his Marine Corps uniform and headed for Camp Lejeune in North Carolina for more training.

He was then shipped to the West Coast to Camp Pendleton in California for further training, then, on another ship, was sent across the ocean to the island of Guadalcanal, which had been captured earlier in the war by the Marines and the Army. He was assigned to the 6th Marine Division and went through a lot of training on Guadalcanal.

He remembered going on many marches, giving out salt pills and getting ready for the invasion of Okinawa while there. He carried first aid kits and a carbine rifle, and that his job was simply that when someone was wounded and they call for Corpsman, "I just run or crawl there to give first aid and get them to stop bleeding or whatever I can do."

He carried medical basics in his kit, such as necessary gauze pads and maybe morphine, which "we didn't use very much but used a lot of sulfur and just the basics of stopping bleeding. We were not there to do great medical work but to save troops and get them back to normal as best we could." Steve was a Pharmacist Mate Third Class and was eventually promoted to Pharmacist Mate Second Class.

He recalled one interesting thing about Guadalcanal: the troops became intrigued with coconuts. "We ate too many and got sick and we never touched them ever again," he offered.

Mail call was always important, and they all lived for it. "It was nice to hear from the family, and I kept up fairly decent correspondence with them," he said. He was single then, but had several girlfriends and also wrote to his buddies who were serving in Europe and were fighting the war there. "We corresponded back and forth—mail call is tremendously important because it was a sign of hope to hear from them on the other side of the world."

The troops sailed out of Guadalcanal about a week prior to the invasion of Okinawa, which was one of the most impressive Easter Sundays that he had ever seen. Ships were there as far as the eye could see, including the Japanese kamikaze planes that were flying suicide missions into the ships. "We went into the northern end of the island not knowing what we were going to face when we got there. For some reason, the Japanese had gone to the other end of the island and there was minimal resistance, but as we traveled south, it got worse and worse and worse." He was assigned to a Pioneer Company that supplied the front lines and he was involved in the combat around Sugarloaf Hill, one of the most difficult battles on Okinawa.

Some units had 100-percent casualties and "many of us in Pioneer Companies were replacements for those line troops. I've been told, and I don't how to prove it, but four Corpsman had been wounded or killed prior to me arriving and I was a fifth one. The interesting thing is that if I got to Sugarloaf Hill earlier, I would've been either killed or wounded like they were, it was a very tough job."

A lot of the island occupants and families were indoctrinated and were told the American Marines were monsters going to rape and kill them, so the locals chose to kill themselves rather than be apprehended. Many of them jumped off the high cliffs into the deep water below.

About the end of June, the island was secured and the Okinawans that survived got a different impression of American troops, that they were not monsters or killers. They found they were truly kind and humane to the people and unfortunately many of the Okinawan residents had taken their own lives before they found out how well the Americans would treat them.

"We left Okinawa and went to the island of Guam and we were then preparing for the invasion of Japan—that was the next destination," he said. They were planning on being with the first waves into Japan because of their experiences with combat on Okinawa. But, before they could head towards the Japanese islands for the final invasion, atomic bombs were exploded on the cities of Hiroshima and Nagasaki, and the war was over. Instead of going to Japan for another invasion, he went to China. His duties in China were to repatriate Japanese troops. They collected Japanese arms and the troops were sent back to their homes. For them, the war was over. He spent six months in China, and while there he met Charlie Two Shoes.

Steve remained in China from November 1945 to April 1946. The Marines he was with all had enough points, so he finally came home, where he resumed his medical studies and discovered that it was really not the field for him. He had always gone to church services, sang in the choir and always carried bulletins and Bibles in his sack, so he entered the ministry, which he remained in for 41 years.

He trained for the ministry while attending Boston University, and he and Marilyn graduated together in 1949. They graduated on Monday and got married the following Saturday. According to Steve, "It was really crazy, but it was the way we did it."

While at Boston University Steve had joined the choir and Marilyn was an alto. He sat in the tenor section right behind her. He said he had been singing in choirs his whole life and that is where he met Marilyn, the love of his life.

He and Marilyn raised four children: two girls, Allison and Susan, and two boys, Andrew and Steven. When he retired from the ministry, he and Marilyn decided to move to the Northcountry of New Hampshire, specifically East Haverhill, where Marilyn's parents maintained an 1840 farmhouse, and it was available because both her parents had died.

Steve and Marilyn moved to East Haverhill in 1992 and he said it has been a wonderful experience, where he can grow a few tomatoes and do a bit of golfing and meet a lot of good friends. They now spend winters in Massachusetts and return to their home in New Hampshire at the beginning of each summer.

Steve and Marilyn have both remained active in their community. Steve is active with the local Veterans of Foreign Wars Post, has participated in many July 4th and Memorial Day parades and has been a favored speaker at many public events. Marilyn has been busy with many local projects and was a member of the popular Haverhill Heritage Commission.

During his retirement in East Haverhill, Steve has served several local churches as interim minister in Bradford, Thetford and West Newbury.

TED AUST AND HIS CREW RESCUED THE SURVIVORS OF PT BOAT 109

(2010)

Ted and I sat in his living room on a couple of afternoons in 1999 and he told me of some interesting days from his Navy experiences during World War II. Ted and his family lived on Brushwood Road in North Haverhill about halfway between Route 116 and Route 25 in Pike.

Often Ted and I would get together for a chat at the Haverhill Corner Post Office and he would recount another great story from his days on PT 157 while serving in the South Pacific during the war. He told me he was always amazed by how many people claim to have been on his boat, PT 157, during the rescue of the future President John F. Kennedy.

Ted was a Motorman First Class aboard his Patrol Torpedo Boat and spent most of his time below decks tending to the huge motor. He said his boat was built in late 1942 in New Jersey, which was his home state and where Ted was born November 27, 1922. He and his also two brothers joined the military from their coastal hometown near Toms River. Ted and his brother Henry joined the military about the same time, which was not long after the Japanese bombed Pearl Harbor on December 7, 1941. By January 1942, Ted was on his way to Newport, Rhode Island for Navy training.

Because military planning and campaigns were developing extremely fast in the nation, his boot camp lasted just three weeks. He was sent to motor school in Jacksonville, Florida, then transported back up to Rhode Island for further PT boat training. He had earlier chosen PT boats because he was one of the top 10 students in his class and the best top 10 got to pick where they would like to spend their Navy days.

Ted sailed to Panama and was assigned as a Motorman to PT 157. They loaded their PT Boats onto a big freighter and set out for New Caledonia, where they established a base. It was from there that he operated throughout the chain of islands in the South Pacific, most of the islands being inhabited by Japanese troops.

Ted told me the night Kennedy's PT boat got sliced in half, a group of their boats went up the coast because they had reports that a Japanese evacuation was going on. He said there were four PT boats in the group: "We were the second boat in line and Kennedy was on the fourth boat."

When they rounded the bend, they could see there was activity on the shore and spotted the silhouettes of a couple of Japanese destroyers. The PT boats received orders to run in and torpedo them, and just about the time the boats fired off a torpedo, the destroyers turned on their searchlights, found the PT boats and started shelling them.

"My job on the boat at that time was to work with the torpedo tubes," Ted noted. "You had to hit the firing pin on the firing mechanism every time they hit an electric switch up in the cockpit, so the launch did not fail. Just as I did that, the Japanese shell landed near our boat and the wave rocked us. My knee went up against the hot torpedo tube and burned me. I thought I had been hit, so we got out of there fast because once you shoot your torpedoes, you are defenseless in the water."

Ted continued, "We had to replace the boats that we lost that night. When we were ready, we took off and went back out to the channel and we were out there maybe a mile or so when we saw a huge explosion south of us. It was unbelievable. It lit up the whole sky and it was about 500 feet in the air with flames everywhere. We wondered what the hell that was.

"By the time we got the word, there was a cruiser coming down toward us. They started shelling us, and I was on the stern working a smoke generator. The skipper said to haul it out to let out a puff of smoke every time a shell lands. They came up our way and the skipper would zig one way and zag the other way to avoid the shells coming in at us. They were closing in on us pretty good, and finally the skipper says to break radio silence and call a base and tell them to intercept the Japanese boat. The Japanese must have picked up the message, because they promptly turned around and headed off in another direction. They were all after us pretty hard by then."

On another night, his PT Boats were sent out to intercept a Japanese squadron coming up the coast, but they did not tell them where the Japanese destroyers were. He said they were just cruising along at a moderate speed and all of a sudden, he heard shouting up on deck and a lot of gun firing going on. "I could not tell what was going on," he said.

"By that time, a slug hit the supercharger of the starboard engine. The supercharger is a fan that forces air when the motor is revved up and now there were gas fumes pouring all over the place. I ran and turned off all the gas lines and the power to the engine. I and tried to get someone on the intercom—all I could hear was mass confusion. I stuck my head out of the hatch and to me it looked like the Fourth of July with tracers crisscrossing above us.

"We lost contact with the other boats immediately and we are just putting along on two engines, and we saw this target up ahead along the beach and we could see the silhouette of a Japanese destroyer. We decided to make a torpedo run on the boat which is a little tricky with only two engines. I could see the torpedoes hit the destroyer and saw the underwater bursts go up in the air, so I knew we hit the damn thing, and we had to get out of there fast." He said they got back to the base well after daylight and everybody was on the dock very worried and waiting for them to return.

On August 1, 1943, PT 157 and crew commanded by Ensign William Liebenow left their base and went to find the crew of PT 109 commanded by John Kennedy, whose ship was disabled and sank after was sliced in two by the Japanese destroyer Amagiri. Ted said that two of Kennedy's men were killed in the incident, and that the remaining 11 others, including Kennedy, abandoned ship into the Pacific Ocean. Kennedy and the others swam to an island where they remained until they were rescued a week later. PT 157, with Ted Aust and the crew on board, picked their way among the islands searching for PT 109's survivors and found them on August 7, 1943. Kennedy was on a small boat that had been run out to meet the rescuers. He climbed aboard PT 157 and they all returned to safety.

Ted recounted how his boat took on the PT 109 survivors and brought them back to a safe island. He said it was no different than any other mission and that he recalled seeing the skipper of PT 109 on several occasions and the only thing that he found remarkable was that Kennedy was so skinny. He said they knew the survivors had been through a tough time after the destroyer cut their boat in half, but 9 of the 11 men were in good shape. They were all very tired and slept a lot on the trip back to safety. He told me they knew Skipper Kennedy was from Massachusetts by the way he talked and pronounced his words.

It was all an interesting time in Ted's life, prior to and after the Kennedy rescue. He recounted for me just what happened. During our interviews—all of which I recorded at that time and still do—I asked Ted if he remembered anything special about Kennedy. He told me that he did remember him well and that, as an officer, Kennedy spoke to everyone aboard his PT boat. He said all of his men liked him, but in the Navy, "some of the officers were real bastards."

I asked Ted if he contacted anybody on his boat about the rescue. He answered that he got a letter from his quartermaster on PT 157 after the war, who and asked if Ted had any pictures because he wanted to make up some kind of a folder. The quartermaster then said he was going to publish a book, and he would like Ted to contribute to it.

"I think I told him that I had donated enough, thank you," recalled Ted, "but I sent him all the pictures I had." Ted never heard back from the quartermaster, and that angered him because Ted never was particularly fond of him when he was on the boat. He found out later that the quartermaster inherited a family business and became quite wealthy. and there he was, trying to publish a book and asked Ted for a donation. Ted suspected the book was probably all about himself anyway.

I asked Ted if he ever got invited anywhere as one of Kennedy's rescuers, like the crew of Kennedy's PT 109 were invited to his Inauguration Day Parade. Ted said "nope"—nobody ever mentioned the rescue to him other than the quartermaster on his boat.

I asked Ted if he had read the definitive book about PT 109. He told me he saw the movie and he only read parts of the book, "but I got tired of it—it was just so much bullshit, even Kennedy said there was too much bullshit."

He didn't like the way it showed the rescue because it depicted them wading out to meet Ted on PT Boat 157. Kennedy did not wade out in the water to meet them. He said that when they picked the survivors up they were on shore. "They came out onto this little wooden dock. It was just barely above the water. We picked them up from the dock because we couldn't get that close to shore."

The whole thing was not that much of a big deal because Kennedy "was just another sailor." He found out that his father, Joseph Kennedy, was an ambassador and that Kennedy came from a wealthy family. "But Kennedy never put on airs or anything like that, like some of them did who were from Annapolis." Kennedy would sit down and play poker with them and show them how to cheat.

PT Boat 157 made a lot of special runs, such as the Kennedy rescue, and it seemed like "every time we had a special mission out there, our boat was picked because it was always running well. I think I can take a little pride in that for myself."

Afterwards, Ted Aust continued his escapades in the South Pacific making torpedo runs and reconnaissance missions until he was rotated out of the area and eventually returned home after the war ended in 1945.

Ted kept in contact with the skipper of his PT 157, Ensign William Liebenow, who would live to be 97 years old. The ensign died in February 2017.

Ted died in Haverhill at age 82 in 2003. He was an interesting and very modest man who took part in dangerous wartime missions and lived to tell about it. Ted told me Kennedy always downplayed the events surrounding the sinking of his boat, but later, others brought the event out to the public with articles in national newspapers and books. He recalled speaking with book authors and writers about that night that he and others on his boat picked up the crew of PT 109 and took them to safety.

After the conclusion of my interviews, Ted wrote me a letter explaining even more about himself and the crew of PT 157. He said war duty was not all serious life or death activities among the Japanese-held islands. He wrote that the boats did not usually go out during the day, but did their real work at night. He wrote that one night he fell off his boat and was not a very good swimmer. He said he was very scared, that he could not get back aboard the 80-foot-long boat, which was 9 feet high in most places except at the rear.

He wrote that he swam to the rear of the boat and somehow managed to haul himself up onto one of the mufflers and climb on deck. "Whew!! I was pooped and soaked." He recalled in his letter. "No one ever heard me until I dropped into the crew quarters, dripping water all over. Boy, did I take a ribbing. I never was a good swimmer and I thought, what the hell am I doing in the Navy?"

He also wrote that "there were always a lot of little activities going on, as we usually stayed in the base area during the day and patrolled at night, except on some special missions. I could go on and on. (signed) T."

"Special missions"—perhaps the special mission they went on and picked up a future president of the United States and his crew. Pretty special for this North Haverhill Sailor.

THREE HAVERHILL BROTHERS ENTERED THE SERVICE TO FIGHT IN WORLD WAR II

(2019)

The third one of those brothers, Raymond, was killed in action and is buried with his fellow infantrymen in the Margraten Military Cemetery in the Netherlands.

As I continue with the Memorial Day series featuring area World War II military service personnel during the war, I spoke with family members of Staff Sergeant Raymond H. Aremburg of Haverhill, who served and fought in World War II.

The Aremburg family is no stranger to military service. During World War II, three brothers were either drafted or signed up for service during the war. They included Raymond in the US Army, with Earl and Rodney Aremburg joining the US Navy. They were three of the seven sons of Roy and Evelyn Aremburg of Haverhill. The four other brothers in the Aremburg family were Lawrence, Charles, Daniel and John. There were also four sisters: Fern, Alice, Marion and Carolyn.

US Army Staff Sergeant Raymond Aremburg was killed in action in Germany on November 29, 1944. Raymond was born in Shelburne, Vermont in August 1923 and attended schools there and in Haverhill. He entered the service November 1942.

Raymond completed his basic training in Texas and was later assigned to the 407th Infantry, 102nd Division. He landed in France sometime after the D-Day invasion of June 6, 1944, fighting his way through France, Belgium, the Netherlands and eventually into Germany. The attack into Germany and the fight to the Roer River kicked off on November 29, 1944. Units of the 102nd Infantry headed to Welz, Linnich and Flossdorf from the border area of the Netherlands and Germany during the closing months of the war.

A fellow soldier, also engaged in the same action that took Aremburg's life on November 29 in furious fighting in the region of the Roer River in Germany, described in a letter how he and a group of soldiers were part of a team that had been pinned down by enemy fire. He said he had witnessed shelling and the burning of six American tanks, and had heard a sniper in the area where he was hiding. He said he lay there very quiet until it became dark and sought protection from a pile of dirt because he was somewhat protected from enemy fire, but with darkness he felt it was best get out of there and head back towards the rear of the action.

He turned and made his way out. He said that the group that stayed in that vicinity against his advice were captured by the Germans. He wrote, "As it became much darker, I decided to crawl back to the rear. The Krauts could not see me, and their sniper was dead. I started to crawl back and everyone I passed was dead. My very good friend, "Dutch" Aremburg (Raymond H.), was slumped over the foxhole he was attempting to dig before he was shot and killed. I kept crawling towards the crest of the hill where our attack was supposed to have stopped."

Raymond Aremburg lies forever in the only American cemetery in the Netherlands. It is located in the village of Magraten. A tall single memorial tower can be seen prior to reaching the 65-acre site. From the cemetery entrance, a visitor would be led to the Court of Honor with its pool reflecting the tall tower. To the right and left there are the visitor buildings and a museum containing three large engraved maps and the stories depicting military operations of the American Armed Forces as they went through the area.

Stretching along the sides of the court are two walls dedicated to those missing in action. Recorded on the walls are the names of 1,722 service members who also gave their lives in the service of their country. Beyond the tower containing the chapel, there is the burial area divided into 16 plots, where 8,301 military dead rest, their headstones set in long curves. A wide tree-lined mall leads to the flagstaff that crowns the crest of the cemetery.

The Aremburg family is well known in the North Country area, and Raymond's brother Earl lives in North Haverhill. I spoke with Earl shortly before this column was written and he told me that Raymond was drafted in November 1942. His other brother in the service, Rodney, went into the Navy in the same year. Earl joined the Navy in 1943.

Earl and his brother Rodney were home on a 30 day leave in early December 1944 when their mother received a telegram informing the family that Raymond was missing in action at that time. During the years he and Raymond were in the service, he never had a chance to see Raymond because when he was home, Raymond was away, and it was always the same.

Earl's brother Rodney was a ship's cook and served in the Pacific. Earl served as a gunner in the Atlantic and Mediterranean areas. When the V-E Day peace document was signed marking the end of the war in Europe on May 8, 1945, he was then sent into the South Pacific to fight the continuing war there (plus, there was anticipation of a major troop landing in Japan, which hopefully would have ended the war).

Before that could happen, the United States dropped two atomic bombs on the cities of Hiroshima and Nagasaki. Peace papers were signed and the war against Japan was over. World War II came to an end on August 14, 1945.

Several years ago, Tammy Fortier, daughter of Wayne and Sandy Fortier of Woodsville, visited Earl's brother Raymond's grave site at the Margraten, Netherlands American Cemetery. She gave him some photos of the site. Other area people have also visited the grave site where Raymond lies.

Had Raymond Aremburg not been killed that November day in 1944, he could have looked forward to pushing on through Germany with his unit, and on May, 3 1945, would have seen and perhaps have actually participated in the historic handshake between members of his 102nd Infantry and the Russian 156th Division when they came together on the outskirts of Berlin, Germany.

That meeting was just five days before the end of the war with Germany.

A PRISONER OF WAR CEREMONY REMINDED ME OF WELLS RIVER'S BILL WHITE

(2018)

Bill White was a survivor of the brutal Bataan Death March and enslavement in Japanese coal mines during World War II. He was finally awarded his Bronze Star Medal prior to his death.

Recently, New Hampshire recognized the sacrifices of 61 Granite State servicemen who died while in captivity during World War II and the Korean War. Many of these and other World War II deaths in captivity took place in the infamous death camps and during long suffering marches undertaken by American, Australian and Filipino prisoners during their long Japanese captivity in the opening part of the war in early 1942.

One man who survived the deadly ordeal was Bill White of Wells River, a man I knew who told me of the experiences he suffered during the Bataan Death March and later as a prisoner and coal mine slave in Japan. For him and many others, it all began when an estimated 65,000 to 80,000 American and Filipino troops were ordered to surrender to invading Japanese forces. The surrendered troops were forced to march from Maraveles at the southern end of Bataan to San Fernando in the middle of Luzon. Those who were weakened from illness or malnutrition were summarily shot or bayoneted, while others who could not keep up with the pace fell out of the formation and were left to die.

The Bataan Death March began in April 1942, after the battle of Bataan in the Philippines. with a total distance marched to the final destination at Camp O'Donnell about 70 miles. Prior to the March, prisoners were ordered to turn over their personal gear and possessions to the Japanese, who kept anything of value for themselves.

Bill White, a Rutland, Vermont, boy, served a total of five and one-half years as a member of the US Army Air Forces serving in the Philippines and in Japan as a prisoner of war. He was stationed at the Bataan Airfield prior to the opening of World War II.

During many conversations I had with Bill, he told me Japanese soldiers herded small groups of Americans together with the prisoners laying out all of their personal gear such as wallets, coins and photographs in front of them. The Japanese kept the jewelry and other things of value. After the wholesale robberies were complete, the Japanese took selected officers and enlisted men behind buildings and executed them.

Word was quickly passed that the men who were summarily executed had possessed Japanese souvenirs and money. That meant for prisoners to conceal or get rid of any Japanese money or mementos because the Japanese captors would know that it had been stolen from dead Japanese soldiers killed by the Americans.

The column of troops marched in unrelenting heat and suffered throughout the entire distance with intensified brutality of the Japanese soldiers who guarded them all along the way. Japanese General Masaharu Homma had earlier issued orders to his officers that American captives should be executed along the way. Some Japanese officers ignored those orders, but other officers were eager to comply with the general's wishes. They murdered many Americans while en route to their prison camps.

Bill White, in describing a small part of his war service, told me they received very little food and almost no water, and that as they proceeded along the march, many died by simply collapsing on the road or they would give up and sit down and await their execution that always came. They marched in sweltering sunlight without helmets or any head covering, and many were shoeless. Many of the troops were arbitrarily stabbed with bayonets, beaten to death or were killed in their attempts to escape or rest.

At the conclusion of the Bataan Death March, prisoner of war Bill White was contained in a prison camp known as Cabanatuan, where he and thousands of others struggled to stay alive while working farm details, clearing land and growing camotes, cassava, taro, sesame and various greens. The prisoners worked six days a week, from 7 AM to 5 PM, and had Sunday off. This daily routine lasted until July 4, 1944, when Bill and 1,000 other prisoners were loaded aboard Japanese ship *Sehiiko Maru*, formerly named *Canadian Inventor*, and sailed to Eastern Japan.

Bill told me that when they reached their final destination, before being put onto ships that would transport them to Japan, they figured conditions would be better, but aboard the Hell Ships, as they were called by the troops, the heat and the crammed bodies in the holds of the ships took its toll and many died along the route.

If they didn't die in the ship's holds, they died at sea. American submarines were plying the waters and were sinking ships filled with American prisoners on their way to Japan to be enslaved for the remainder of the war.

The American submarine commanders were unaware that many of the old Japanese freighters headed toward Japanese ports did not contain war materials to help Japan fight the war, but they were filled with human cargo—American GIs who had become prisoners of war.

Total deaths from the Bataan Death March were set between 6,000 and 8,000, with more dying from a variety of diseases that crippled the troops, including inhumane, criminal behavior and treatment of the prisoners by the Japanese guards who accompanied them along the way.

According to the history of the Bataan and Corregidor Death March Survivors Association and the United States Army Air Forces accounting of the area during that period of early 1942, the situation for the USAAF personnel was hopeless, with the men surrendering only when they were ordered to do so by their commanding officers. Many would have preferred to keep fighting, with some chance of survival.

After the surrender, many USAAF men paid the ultimate price during the brutal and infamous attend Death March or in the miserable conditions of Japanese imprisonment later. As many as 11,000 prisoners of war died, and over twice as many POWs died in the first two months of imprisonment at another prison, Camp O'Donnell.

Thousands died later in these and other POW camps throughout the war, with more succumbing on the so-called Hell Ships. Although it is difficult to establish exactly what happened to all of the US Army Air Forces pilots and enlisted personnel on Bataan, the record shows that of 1,144 enlisted men in the US Army Air Forces at the start of the fighting, 16 were evacuated, 38 were killed and the remainder became POWs, of whom over 60 percent died in captivity. Bill White somehow managed to live through it all.

Bill was liberated from the Japanese and left Japan on the US Ship Simon Bolivar. He arrived in San Francisco on October 21, 1945, and on January 1, 1946, he married his sweetheart, Martha Metcalf, in Vermont. He graduated from the Rutland, Vermont, Business College in 1949, and in 1951, the couple moved to Wells River, where he became a successful banker and businessman. In 1953, Bill was hired by the Wells River Savings Bank and retired as the executive vice president in 1972. He and Martha then entered business and purchased the Wells River Motel, which he successfully operated until 1978.

Bill was also deeply involved with his community. He was a past president of the Wells River–Woodsville Rotary Club, and was a deacon, the treasurer and a member of the board of trustees of the Wells River Congregational Church. He was a trustee of Cottage Hospital and an honored member of the Ross Wood Post 20, American Legion and the Disabled American Veterans, and was a life member of the American Defenders of Bataan and Corregidor.

He and I enjoyed talking about military subjects. He revealed to me that, although President Harry Truman had authorized the award of The Bronze Star to all the Bataan Death March survivors, he was told that if he wanted his award, he was required to travel to Camp Devens in Massachusetts to pick it up.

He said if the Army really cared about getting him the award, they would find someone somewhere to present the medals to the survivors. He had no intention of driving all the way down to Massachusetts from his home in Vermont to pick up his medal. He said he would rather go without. That is the kind of pride Bill had. I admired him immensely.

After he revealed to me that he would never go to Massachusetts to pick up his Bronze Star, I thought it would be appropriate to find someone who would bring the Bronze Star to Bill. The next day, I contacted US Senator Patrick Leahy's (D-VT) office to tell them the story, and if the senator or someone—anyone—in Washington, DC, might find a way to get Bill his medal.

They agreed he should receive the medal, but to do that, they said they would need all his paperwork from his World War II service and captivity. This assignment was no easy task, especially since I was working on the sly to get him his medal as a surprise. His wonderful wife, Martha, cooperated with my efforts to get the required information, and she surreptitiously slipped me all the documents, his DD-214 and other important papers needed by Senator Leahy to verify the military facts from so long ago.

Some time later, Senator Leahy's office called back and notified me that Bill had been selected to earn the medal and the senator wanted to pin it on him as soon as possible. We settled on a Memorial Day ceremony in 1987 that was to be held at the Happy Hour Restaurant in Wells River.

Martha kept the secret. I invited a world of veterans' organizations and friends of Bill and Martha, plus all the media I could think of. We even had a band there to play military music.

On the appointed day, Bill White walked into the Happy Hour Restaurant to the glare of television lights and camera strobe units and met Senator Leahy, other national and local politicians, friends, fellow veterans and business associates who watched as Bill White stood at attention and had his long-deserved Bronze Star Medal pinned on his chest by US Senator Leahy.

It was a glorious day and Bill White was finally presented with the medal that he had suffered so long for. It was a proud day and it was good to see Bill smile and be happy with an occasion that brought together family, friends and neighbors to celebrate his extreme heroism.

Bill White died in 1992, but before he died, a grateful nation was able to show him how proud it was of his brave service and devotion our country.

KENNETH FULLER SERVED IN WORLD WAR II

(2020)

His wife Marilyn told me all about Ken and his service to our country. Ken served nearly four years away from home during World War II and was proud to have done that.

While at the recent craft fair held at the Haverhill Cooperative Middle School, I saw many friends in the crowd that visited this wonderful pre-Christmas event. One of those was my dear friend Marilyn Fuller from Newbury. She was there with many of her friends and I would say she knew most of the visitors who came through the door. She was like the Mayor of the Craft Fair, and it was great to see her once again.

I have always been interested in Marilyn's husband Ken's World War II service, something he and I talked about from time to time. She promised she would get me the facts of all that he did during the war. Always true to her word, not long ago I received a letter in her familiar handwriting. It contained dates and times of Ken's Army years from 1942 to 1946. I am sure she knows this information by heart.

As for Marilyn, she served many years with the 4-H, working with kids from throughout the area. She was always involved with the community in many ways and I think I've interviewed her 20 times over the years about her various projects she was participating in with her 4-H students. Whenever I met with Marilyn for an interview or went to look at one of her many projects, she was always with her husband Kenneth Fuller, a wonderful man who served his country during World War II. Ken and Marilyn were selected several years

World War II veteran Ken Fuller and his wife, Marilyn, of Newbury, Vermont, are well known personalities in the Vermont region of Ryegate and beyond. Here, Ken and Marilyn are seen at a Woodsville–Wells river July 4th Parade after Ken was honored by being named Grand Marshal. Image credit *The Bridge Weekly*, Bernie Marvin.

ago to be Parade Marshals with the Woodsville–Wells River July 4th Parade.

Ken spent four years away serving with the US Army in a variety of places, but mainly with the Signal Corps in Hawaii, and later the South Pacific. He was attached to the 101st Signal Battalion, Company C, and participated in the Battle of Saipan in 1944.

Marilyn told me he also went to Leyte in the Philippine Islands and participated in the Battle of Leyte. After all that, he prepared for the final battle of World War II at the island of Okinawa, located just off the coast of Japan. She said his company was issued all new equipment, new jeeps and trucks, Bulldozers and landing vessels for the battle of Okinawa. The Okinawa campaign began April 1, 1945. Marilyn said Kenneth had a lot of close calls, many air raids, Japanese artillery and many snipers. After the landings on Okinawa, Ken's biggest job was to install underground telegraph and telephone cables near the airstrip.

The war was finally over after the atomic bombs were dropped and Ken was shipped back to the United States and discharged at Fort Devens, Massachusetts, on January 1, 1946. He made it home to Newbury Center for a grand welcome home celebration.

She told me that Ken wrote to his mother often from the front in the form of V-Mail and regular mail before he got "into the thick of it." Marilyn said Ken was always proud of his service to his country and always wore his veterans cap identifying him as a "World War II veteran."

He married Marilyn on February 4, 1950, and together they farmed the Maple Cream Farm in Newbury Center. He also owned Ken's Texaco in North Haverhill. He retired in 1998 at 77 years of age. He died August 1, 2012.

Marilyn told me that Ken's uniforms were given to a grandson who served in Iraq and also served 12 years in the National Guard. He was based at the Littleton Armory.

For many Veterans Days, I could always count on a nice handwritten note and a Thank You card from Marilyn Fuller. I know she sent these sweet notes to others, as well, because she has a host of friends around the area who knew her and Ken as patriotic people who took time to remember others, especially their veteran friends.

KEN ULINE OF LYME IS A WORLD WAR II TANKER AND SURVIVOR OF D-DAY.

(2020)

Ken Uline, 93, is Lyme's oldest resident. He left his town to join the US Army, returned after the war and never left again. He is a 1st Armored Division veteran and proud of it!

World War II veteran Ken Uline of Lyme, New Hampshire, has received many honors in his life, such as being named Lyme Citizen of the Year by the Lyme Foundation, plus being named twice as Memorial Day Parade Marshal in the nearby town of Piermont. Piermont selects area veterans for this honor to highlight their service to their country and their community.

During the Piermont Memorial Day Parade of 2019, Ken Uline, dressed smartly in his World War II uniform, complete with patches and ribbons, was applauded throughout his ride in an authentic US Army Jeep as it rolled proudly along Church Street, onto Routes 25 and 10, where the Piermont Memorial Day Parade terminated at the Piermont Veterans Memorial Garden.

Ken is a favorite in Piermont. Last year he—accompanied by his two daughters, Betsy and Nancy—proceeded throughout the Memorial Day program that was dedicated to the memory of all the fallen members of our US Armed Forces.

Jeff Valence of the Lyme Foundation wrote, in his description of Ken during the presentation of the coveted Lyme Citizen of the Year, that Ken served in the United States Army 1st Armored Division during World War II, "a fact of great significance in his life and yet a subject he shares with reservation and humility."

I have selected parts of Mr. Valence's tribute and introduction of Ken prior to the Lyme Citizen of the Year Award; Mr. Valence said the 1st Armored Division was "engaged in some of the bloodiest and significant battles in the European Theater of World War II. His service represents a sense of responsibility to serve others, even to the extent that it would require his own life. In Stuttgart, Germany, where he served, a memorial to his unit's and others' service reads, 'If you were not here, then we would not be now.'"

Mr. Valence continued, "Service of this kind is what permits us today to ponder what it means in this small town in rural New Hampshire. Versatility, ingenuity and self-reliance; humility, service to others and self-sacrifice; love and commitment of one's home and family.

"These traits and his long service to Lyme are worthy of praise, however, it is his universal kindness, generosity and warmth that are most notable because these are the traits that make Lyme unique. As much as volunteering and service is vital to our town, the routine simple acts of kindness that are shared make Lyme a place that is special to so many.

"It is in the simple act of a wave each time you pass by his house. It is in the fact, once you have the courage to finally stop the car and say 'hello,' that he welcomes you with a smile, a story and the feeling that no matter how long you have lived in Lyme or where you live in Lyme, he shows you what it means to be a neighbor—the way it has been in Lyme, and those of us who are newcomers, if we follow his example, what Lyme can continue to be.

"He represents versatility and work ethic—wonderful examples of which trace back as far as his early youth, as a young child and youngest of seven children, he was responsible to change the lights of the church clock, which was accomplished by tying a rope around his waist and being hauled up three stories by hand (without his mother knowing it)."

Ken Uline, a World War II Tanker of Lyme, New Hampshire, is a popular icon in New Hampshire's Upper Valley region, where he has lived all his life, except for time spent fighting in Europe. Often on warm summer days, Ken can be seen in his comfortable chair on his front lawn waving to passing friends from throughout the area. He is lovingly cared for at home by his two daughters, Betsy and Nancy. Image credit: *The Bridge Weekly*, Bernie Marvin.

Ken was involved in the establishment of one of the symbols of Lyme that, Valence claims, is now taken for granted: Chase Beach. Ken helped construct the boat launch at Reservoir Pond, was a regular on the fire department as a young boy and later served as First Assistant Chief. He helped clear timber out of Mud Pond that accumulated there in 1938 when a windstorm dropped 4.2 million board feet of trees in Lyme.

"He cut 47 cord of wood each winter by hand with his father, brothers, and sisters," wrote Valence. "Climbed nearly every hill and valley in Lyme, and when he wanted to see a movie—at the only place in the Upper Valley where one could do such a thing, the Lebanon

Opera House—he rode his bike (a one-speed) the entire distance with his friend riding on the handlebars.

"His careers demonstrate the ingenuity and self-reliance of those that lived before us. He was a soldier, electronics technician, construction worker, tile mason, handyman and source of advice for many residents when they needed something repaired or built on their property, as well as a father, husband and friend to many. Like so many of our early citizens, he was skilled at many trades, but appreciated the artistic side of life. In the case of our Citizen of the Year, he is exceptionally talented with the tenor banjo, mandolin and guitar.

"What makes Lyme special?" Valence asks. "It is that we place greater importance on community than on convenience. It is the routine acts of kindness that are shown; it is the example of our town's heritage; it is in the act that one takes the time to wave and one takes the time to notice, and we take the time to appreciate. It is that you can say that among our citizens we can call Ken Uline one of our own."

Valence concludes, "It is with great privilege and honor that I can at introduce this year's Citizen of the year, Kenneth Hiram Uline."

IT WAS A NIGHT OF "ROCKETS' RED GLARE, THE BOMBS BURSTING IN AIR"

(2016)

Piermont residents paid tribute to the late World War II veteran Bill Simpson and his fellow veterans who served their country and their town since the days of the French and Indian War.

It was a spectacular light show in the late summer sky as 21 minutes of fireworks were launched upwards to celebrate the life and heroism of Piermont veterans who have served their country and town since the closing days of the French and Indian War back in 1763. Saturday night, August 22, was the first military veterans' appreciation event held in town and it was a total success with food, special music and spectacular fireworks.

The special evening took place at the recently constructed Piermont Veterans Memorial Garden inside the South Lawn Cemetery that was created to show the town's appreciations to its veterans and their service to America and New Hampshire since the French and Indian War that ended a year prior to the town's charter, which was granted in 1764. From that early war through the years to the present time, Piermonters have fought and died in nearly every war and most combat actions since then.

The card of events for the nearly 200 visitors who showed up for the program included a chicken barbecue prepared by 15 members of the Piermont Fire Department, a meal that included their specially sauced chicken and all the fixings and more. Also featured throughout the program, which began at 6 PM and concluded at 9:30 PM, was a wide range of traditional patriotic music and military marches played by the Mad Bavarian Brass Band under the baton of Bill Sharp. Capping off the night was a long fireworks display sent aloft by North Star Fireworks Company of East Montpelier, Vermont.

The event is named in honor of the late William Simpson, a Marine Corps veteran of World War II and a survivor of amphibious landings on the Marshal Islands, plus the island campaigns of Saipan, Tinian and Iwo Jima. Bill was wounded at Iwo Jima and spent nearly a year in the hospital recovering. He was awarded the Purple Heart Medal for his wounds. He died on Thursday, August 20, just two days prior to Saturday night's BBQ, concert and fireworks. Many of Bill and his beloved wife Ellen's friends attended the dinner and recalled his wonderful sense of humor, his dedicated patriotism and his amazing work ethic that never ran out, even as he enjoyed life during his 90th year.

Bill and Ellen had been married 69 years and raised two daughters, Karen and Julie. I have attended town meetings in Piermont for many years, whether to cover them for local newspapers or to vote there during the past nine years, and always sitting at left center of the school gym were Bill and Ellen, listening attentively and voting with enthusiasm. There was never a program in town that Bill did not have a hand in, from farming to construction, to painting, to fund raising, to volunteering his time to the Piermont Fire Department, where he served many years. He was also one of the many carpenters and others who worked hard to construct the present fire station, still in use located just south of the Four Corners.

As part of two recent annual Memorial Day parades featured in this town, Bill Simpson rode along as part of the student float that depicted the Marine Corps War Memorial flag raising at Iwo Jima. For another parade, he was selected at the Memorial Day Parade

Marshal and he rode the route to the cheers and applause of parade watchers along the way.

And so, in his memory and for those other veterans who have served their country and community, last Saturday's event was dedicated to those unselfish people, who for so long have fought our wars and paid the price. They were honored for all that, as they will be each year in the future on a late summer or early fall day, when the town gathers for a BBQ, a concert and fireworks that will be dedicated to the towns veterans, first responders and volunteers.

NEIGHBORS AND FRIENDS TEND OUR OVERSEAS CEMETERIES

(2019)

A local soldier, Raymond Cole, was killed during his ascent of Pont du Hoc on the Normandy Beachhead. He remains there forever, in the American Cemetery in Normandy.

As Memorial Day approaches, *Bernie's Beat* column continues with stories on area veterans who fought and died during World War II. They will be remembered by many during the upcoming Memorial Day services occurring throughout our region.

According to notes sent to me by the American Battle Monuments Commission, by the end of World War II several hundred temporary burial grounds had been established on battlefields around the world. In 1947, 14 sites in foreign countries were selected to become permanent burial grounds by the American Battle Monuments Commission. The locations of the sites corresponded closely with the course of military operations during the war.

After the war, all temporary World War II cemeteries were discontinued by the War Department. Cemeteries for World War II dead were then were established throughout Europe as permanent military burial grounds and granted by the host country in perpetuity. Each grave site is within a permanent American World War I and II Cemetery on foreign soil and is marked by headstones of white marble. In addition to their landscaped grave areas and nonsectarian chapels, the World War II cemeteries contain sculpture, a visitor reception facility and a museum area with battle maps and narratives depicting the course of the war in the region.

The final resting place for one area American G.I. who participated in the June 6, 1944 D-Day landings is the Normandy Cemetery located on a cliff overlooking Omaha Beach and the English Channel near St. Laurent Sur Mer, about 170 miles west of Paris, France. It was here in the morning of that historic invasion day that Private First Class Raymond A. Cole, born and raised in nearby Landaff, landed on the beach as a member of the US Army 2nd Ranger Battalion. His mission was to scale the hundred-foot vertical cliffs at Pointe Du Hoc that rose near the landing beaches of Normandy.

Sometime during the day of June 6th, it was reported that "Cole's down!" and as the furious action continued for the men of the 2nd Ranger Battalion, casualty rates grew. In the end less, than 90 men of the original 250 that began the assault survived the attack on Pointe Du Hoc.

Private First Class Cole rests forever in the Normandy American Cemetery and Memorial in Normandy, France. At his head stands a white marble cross listing only his name, rank, unit, state of former residence and the date of his death: Raymond A. Cole, PFC, 2d Ranger Bn, New Hampshire, June 6, 1944. That is the story of this Landaff boy's life and death history on D-Day. He landed, he assaulted, and he died, all within that single day.

Private First Class Cole's Nephew, Tim Cole, of Orford and formerly of Piermont, speaks fondly of his Uncle Raymond, although he was very young when Raymond was around the area. Tim Cole's father, Archie, was one of Raymond's seven brothers and sisters who were raised in Landaff, but who moved around to where the work was located.

Archie Cole eventually settled in Piermont on the old Brook Road, now Route 25C, where he and the family tended their farm. Archie, like most young men of that era, either signed up or was drafted into the Army and went off to war. Archie ended up fighting on the Italian front and survived the war.

Archie's spirit of America was passed to son, Tim. He was caught up in the Vietnam War draft and shipped off to Vietnam for his year of duty there. He left the Army after the completion of his three-year hitch and returned to Piermont, where he went on to serve the town as its fire chief for 18 years, among many other jobs he held as a volunteer.

Raymond Cole was 22 years old when he was killed scaling the steep canyon wall of Pointe Du Hoc. He had dutifully reported to the Army just prior to Christmas on December 15, 1942 at Manchester, where, as a civilian, he was a machine shop operator. Raymond was not married and left no dependents according to his documents on file with the Battlefield Commission. Raymond lies within the cemetery where H Row 24, Grave 35 is located.

During the 2019 Piermont, New Hampshire, Memorial Day observance in the Piermont Veterans Memorial Garden, Tim Cole gave a speech about his uncle and the assault on Ponte Du Hoc on the morning of June 6, 1944. He said, "Raymond A. Cole was born in 1922, raised on a farm in New Hampshire and was among the youngest of eight children. He enlisted in the Army on December 15, 1942, at Manchester, New Hampshire. He was employed in a machine shop there, was single and had no dependents.

"The 2nd Ranger Battalion was formed at Camp Forrest, Tennessee, on April 1, 1943, along with the 5th Ranger Battalion. Both battalions were officially activated in September 1943 and shipped to Great Britain where they were prepared for the Operation Overlord mission.

"On June 6, 1944—D-Day—they had a most dangerous mission: They landed on Omaha Beach dodging heavy German machine gun fire. They then scaled a cliff while still under intense enemy fire. The job was to take out the big German guns at the top of the cliffs—guns that were trained on the Normandy beaches. Uncle Raymond was in an assault landing craft, Number 883, when he landed at the base of Pont Du Hoc and then climbed to the top on rope ladders carrying heavy loads and his M1 Garand rifle. As he reached the top, he was fatally wounded.

"The Rangers mission was one of the most difficult and daring of the entire invasion: to climb the sheer and desolate cliffs and take out the enemy guns. The Rangers looked up and saw the enemy soldiers at the edge of the cliffs shooting down at them with machine guns, and they were also throwing grenades. The American Rangers shot rope ladders out over the face of the cliffs and began to pull themselves up. When one Ranger fell, another would take his place.

"When one rope was cut, a Ranger would grab another and begin his climb again. They climbed, shot back and held their footing. Soon, one by one, the Rangers pulled themselves over the top and seized the land at the top of these cliffs. They began to take back the continent of Europe. Of the 250 that landed that morning, only 90 were alive after two days of fighting.

"Pfc. Raymond A. Cole (Service Number 31265003) is buried and memorialized in the Normandy American Cemetery, Colleville-Sur-Mer, France. Uncle Raymond was adopted by Marie Pascale-Legrand of Normandy, whom we have met during her trip to America. She and her nephew and niece continue to care for Uncle Raymond's grave.

"My father was First Sgt. Archie Cole, who was four years older than his brother Raymond. He served in the Army and was a Pearl

Harbor survivor. He knew very little about Raymond's death at the time. Uncle Raymond is our family hero, along with all others who serve so valiantly."

The cemetery covers 172 acres and contains the graves of 9,386 military dead, most of whom lost their lives in the landings and ensuing operations after they got off the beachhead at Normandy and proceeded through France.

On the walls of a semicircular garden on the east side of the memorial are inscribed the names of 1,557 missing soldiers who sleep elsewhere in unknown graves. The memorial consists of a semicircular structure containing large maps and narratives of military operations, and at the center is the bronze statue showing the "Spirit of American Youth."

Concerning Private First Class Cole's assault area, the Pointe Du Hoc Ranger Monument is located on a cliff eight miles west of the Normandy American Cemetery and overlooks Omaha Beach. It was erected by the French to honor elements of the 2nd Ranger Battalion that scaled the 100-foot cliff, seized the objective and defended it successfully against determined German counterattacks at a very high cost. A battle-scarred area on the right flank of Omaha Beach remains much as the Rangers left it on June 6, 1944.

Tim Cole told me that his Uncle Raymond's grave is always decorated with homegrown flowers from nearby gardens in Normandy. The flowers are grown by neighbors and placed on graves in the American Cemetery nearby.

As Tim mentioned in his speech, one family that places flowers on American soldiers' graves is that of Marie Pascale-Legrand, who has been doing the honor since 1984, after the mayor of her village asked if she could house a few American soldiers for the 40th anniversary celebration of D-Day. Legrand, on a recent visit to New Hampshire to visit members of the Cole family, said, "We were liberated by the allied forces and I will never forget that. We are free now. It is our duty to honor those who served."

Cole said the Legrands came to New Hampshire to meet with him and his sister Joyce, as well as another family that has a relative buried in the American Cemetery at Normandy. He said the French neighbors in Normandy will continue the tradition of decorating Americans graves forever, as other family members learn about performing these honors to pay tribute and appreciation to the soldiers who saved their country.

RVN, Grunts and Choppers

When the call was made, they answered

MEMORIAL DAY: A TIME FOR CHILDREN TO HEAR ABOUT SERVICE

(2010)

When Selectman, New Hampshire Representative and Piermont's Memorial Day Guest Speaker Rick Ladd stepped forward to address the crowd during the annual Memorial Day Parade and services, youngsters from the Piermont Village School were quite interested in what he was about to tell them.

Earlier in the week, guest speaker Rick Ladd of Haverhill had stopped by a group of combined upper grades at the K–8 school and spoke briefly with them about the significance of what they were embarking on when they created yet another patriotic float for their town's Memorial Day Parade.

For the previous year's parade, the Piermont Village School children recreated the historic World War II flag raising on Mount Surabachi on the island of Iwo Jima and displayed their effort along the parade route to the applause of an appreciative public.

The honored guest on that float was Piermont resident William Simpson, a World War II Marine Corps veteran and Iwo Jima survivor who was wounded during that February 1945 invasion.

Through the years they were in school, the kids continued their patriotic themes, creating a float dedicated to the Tomb of the Unknowns, similar to the monument seen in Arlington National Cemetery. To complete this honor, children worked with their teachers and parents to construct and decorate these floats and accompany them on the parade route.

Vietnam veteran, Lieutenant Rick Ladd of Haverhill, New Hampshire, speaks at an education seminar in his town of Haverhill recently. Ladd is a former town selectman, a precinct commissioner and a longtime member of the New Hampshire House of Representatives. He is active in his community and is a member of Veterans of Foreign Wars Post 5245. Image credit: *The Bridge Weekly*, Bernie Marvin.

During the past several years, the principal and her staff have assisted the children in creating patriotic scenarios, and now with the startup of a school band and chorus, they too have been featured in Memorial Day programs held at the conclusion of the parade at the Piermont Veterans Memorial Garden.

Ladd—a former teacher and school principal in Maine and Alaska before relocating to Haverhill with his wife, Margaret—knows the importance of having children involved with an event as important as Memorial Day. He told them during his appearance at their school he was always pleased to speak with children who wanted to know more about the special day or who wanted to participate in one of America's most meaningful patriotic holidays.

Ladd cited the deaths of Americans through the years going back to the American Revolution up to today's ongoing wars in Iraq and Afghanistan. He told of the losses suffered through all those wars, especially the loss of the citizen soldiers from the various National Guard units that have also fought those wars.

He knows his history and his wars well, as he served in the Vietnam War as an artillery officer and came away from that with three Bronze Stars and an Air Medal for Valor.

Ladd noted that when military topics are discussed, the kids have not heard much about the sacrifices made by a special group of heroes: the members of the Women's Airforce Service Pilots of World War II (WASP).

He said those women pilots all flew more than 60 million miles and lost 38 pilots during the war, flying nearly 40 different types of combat airplanes to units all over the country.

"That's something we don't hear much about when we discuss World War II," Ladd said.

He also noted that several times, when the Dean Memorial Airport Commission held their annual Airport Awareness Day, a number of former members of the Women's Airforce Service Pilots would be a part of those programs, and that in past years the women pilots attended various Airport Awareness Day events and told stories of their flights all over the country during the war. These women also spoke at many local schools in Vermont and New Hampshire.

At a different location, the North Haverhill Memorial Day services featured the Veterans of Foreign Wars unit who remembered one of their own members, Fred Robinson, who had been awarded a Silver Star Medal for his heroic service during World War II.

No one heard much about his service years from Fred during his many devoted years working at the Aldrich General Store, but when one thinks about genuine war heroes, they think about Fred Robinson and other soldiers like him who put down their pitch forks, shovels, pencils or adding machines and went off to fight the war, Ladd told them.

Fred Robinson worked at the Aldrich General Store for more than 50 years and was a founder and charter member. He was also the first Post Commander of the Haverhill Memorial VFW Post 5245 in North Haverhill, and a member of the North Haverhill Volunteer Fire Department for over 25 years.

Fred was born in Haverhill in June 1917 and graduated from Haverhill Academy. He worked for a while at the Dana Fadden farm in Piermont. He served with the US Army during World War II from January 1942—just after the surprise attack by the Japanese at the Pearl Harbor Naval base—through the duration of the war, and was discharged at the end of November 1945.

Fred was with Company A, 114th Combat Engineers that was attached to the 32nd Division in New Guinea and Australia. For his gallant and heroic actions in New Guinea he was presented his Silver Star and a Purple Heart for wounds received.

On two separate occasions, he rescued two wounded soldiers from certain death. The second rescue, which was awfully close to the enemy positions, he was wounded when shot in the shoulder. When Fred was recuperating from his injuries in a military hospital near Sydney, Australia, he met his future wife, Audrey George, on a blind date. They were married in Banks Town, New South Wales, Australia in February 1945. Fred came back home to the town he loved, North Haverhill, and his wife Audrey joined him in the first week of May 1946.

Fred died in February 2011.

Those were a few of the reflections made over the holiday weekend, and it was good for children to see and hear it from those who served and made it home to tell others about their wartime experiences on Memorial Day.

BOOK BY DARTMOUTH VIETNAM WAR VETERANS DESCRIBED AS A REMARKABLE HISTORY

(2014)

The book also features a story by Haverhill Corner veteran Bob Rose. He tells his story of the three years he served in the US Army during the tumultuous times of the Vietnam War.

I was a bit a surprised to read this week about a little kid I knew as the brother of a girl who graduated with me from Winchester High School. Classmate Gretchen Luitwieler's little brother, Peter, I recall vaguely and only that he was part of Gretchen's family.

The book I was reading, *Dartmouth Veterans – Vietnam Perspectives,* is a very good book written by the Class of 1964 Dartmouth grads who went on to join the nation's armed forces, with many of them being sent to Vietnam during those dreadful war years, in a war that began in 1959 and finally came to a close in 1975. Edited by Phillip C. Schaefer with David S. deCalesta, Frederick C. Gray, James P. Stewart and Robert J. Woodruff, it is published by Dartmouth College Press, an imprint of the University Press of New England.

The book is dedicated to three 1964 graduates, all victims of the Vietnam War: US Navy Pilot William Brewster Nickerson, US Air Force Pilot Peter Whitcomb Morrison and US Army Infantryman John Wheeler Griffin, III.

Historian and veteran advocate James Wright and Dartmouth President Emeritus Eleazar Wheelock, Professor of History and a United States Marine, wrote the forward in the book, *Dartmouth Veterans - Vietnam Perspectives.* It is a history written by those military graduates who went off to war, or to a duty station somewhere in the world. Their stories—some long and critically defining, some short and quite to the point—are beautifully executed, each with an update on the writer and where he is now with his life.

A total of 58 stories are presented. Here are some sample titles: "Military Service" by Tom Seymour; "Rolling Thunder: One Small Step to Enlightenment" by Robert B. Field, Jr.; "The Green Lieutenant" by Hugh Savage; "The Maturing of a Dartmouth Marine" by Lee A. Chilcote and "Life in A Jungle Base Camp" by Carl Durei.

Their duty and service writings tell a story of inductions to all branches of the military, some fun, some horrid, but all told with a pride in their uniform and performance that has defined most of them to this day.

Among the authors of written comments on the back cover of *Dartmouth Veterans* was Dartmouth grad Joe Medlicott of Piermont, class of 1950, who came back from World War II combat where he served as a paratrooper with the 82nd Airborne Division. He has spent a lifetime in education and is still educating, now serving as an instructor with the Osher Lifelong Learning Institute at Dartmouth (formerly ILEAD).

Professor Joe writes that the book reminds the reader of what Erich Maria Remarque, the author of the classic *All Quiet on the Western Front*, wrote of his generation: "a generation that was destroyed by the war—even those of it who survived the shelling."

For me, it was like reading a local book, written with a realistic look and feel for military service, especially since I could read about that young Luitweiler boy from Winchester, Massachusetts (where I was born and raised) who grew up to earn a Vietnamese Cross of Gallantry. And to also see a back-cover praise written by my widely respected acquaintance, fellow veteran and Piermont neighbor, Joe Medlicott was a thrill.

But wait, there's more! There's also a story written by my neighbor in Haverhill Corner, Dr. Bob Rose. When we lived there, we were located diagonally across Dartmouth College Highway from Bob and Betsy. He was a 1968 graduate from the University of Wisconsin Medical School. Dr. Rose was drafted into the Army obtained a reserve commission and then a residency in anesthesiology at Dartmouth. Dr. Bob spent the majority of his three years of service with the US Army's 1st Infantry Division at Fort Riley, Kansas. He reported, as did most who wrote their accounts for the book, that his military service was a positive experience and he felt privileged to have served.

The book is great reading. If you thought all those "Smart Aleky College Boys" spent their time in the "O" Club eating great chow and drinking chilled martinis, while us enlisted swine hunkered down in the mud and ate "C Rats," I am here to tell you it wasn't that way at all, at least according to the book. Although most of them could have avoided the whole mess, they signed up and served. They own stock in America and the country owes them gratitude and thanks.

While I have the chance, this Jarhead will now echo what many people tell me these days. I am proud to pass it on to those 1964 Dartmouth grads who raised their right hands way back when.

THE VIETNAM WAR MEMORIAL WALL APPEARANCE WAS AN IMPORTANT EVENT

(2010)

It was a busy and meaningful six-day schedule and included many veterans and civic organizations coming to North Haverhill offering praise and emotion for the war survivors.

From the opening escort of emergency vehicles and motorcycles on Wednesday, to the closing retrieval of colors by veterans' groups on Monday afternoon this week, the visit by the Vietnam War Memorial Wall was an event filled with impact, emotion and friendship.

From the beginning and throughout each day, I witnessed countless acts of emotion and comradeship, as veterans, their families, those in the emergency services—including police, fire and emergency medical personnel—and thousands of others came to the wall to see the nearly 59,000 names of combat dead and missing listed on panels that measure 80 percent of the size of the original Vietnam War Memorial in Washington, DC.

The weather cooperated, sort of, and except for rain on Saturday and Sunday morning, crowds packed the exhibits that included The Wall and tributes to those who fought and died in both world wars; combat actions around the globe; September 11, 2001, terrorist attacks and also deaths of serving members of law enforcement, firefighting and emergency medical services.

There were many highlights over the six days that I visited The Wall exhibits and spoke with many who had traveled there from far away to see family and friends' names appearing on The Wall. In many instances, personal tributes and flowers were left at many panels along the entire length of The Wall.

The Wall travels the nation. The exhibit, once it is taken down and packed away in the truck for transport, will then travel to Kansas. The Wall that appeared for six days in North Haverhill is the largest traveling wall in America and is 8 feet at its highest point and 370 feet long. Veterans Wayne Fortier and Robert Williams served as co-coordinators of this massive project that saw several daily and evening programs that involved a host of people from around the Twin-State region.

The names etched on gold-colored dog tags of those killed while serving the nation since the end of the Vietnam War, including Iraq and Afghanistan, are an interesting display, and this display is continually updated.

A visit to the location provided a complete story of just what it takes for a country to remain free. This is why so many schools continually visited The Wall location, with some, such as the Haverhill Cooperative Middle School and the Warren Village School students, sitting as a respectful audience as the rains fell during one program.

Featured for all to see and learn from were casualty reports from the American Revolution, War of 1812, Indian Wars, Mexican War, the Spanish–American War and the Civil War, with losses accounted for from both the north and south.

Also included were numbers of casualties from World War I, World War II, the Korean War, the Vietnam War and Desert Storm. A sobering fact is that serving all of these conflicts throughout the world, a total of 34,187,907 Americans donned the uniform to serve and fight and die.

It was both an honor and privilege to walk the fairgrounds and speak with visitors who had questions of how to find names of their loved ones or friends. The Name Location Center computer installation was a superb part of this exhibit and provided visitors with interesting information about the names upon The Wall.

Everyone I spoke with throughout the six days of observing the exhibits while photographing the events was pleased and impressed by this outstanding program produced by members and leadership of the North Haverhill Post 5245, Veterans of Foreign Wars and the Woodsville Ross–Wood Post 20 of the American Legion. These members served as guides and ushers, and were always available to answer important questions. They directed traffic, provided impressive flag details, drove or escorted elderly visitors around the exhibits and showed compassion and caring when visitors' emotions were shattered when they saw a loved one's name etched on a panel that was part of this outstanding American Veterans Traveling Tribute.

It was an exhibit about the cost of freedom and was an important reminder for us all.

JOHN O'BRIEN BATS A FENWAY HOME RUN FOR VETERANS

(2018)

Orford forester and well-known veteran John O'Brien received an outstanding Father's Day surprise from his three children while at a Red Sox game on June 22, 2018.

Little did O'Brien know, but he had more in store for him that day than just a Red Sox game. During the game and again during an inning break, the announcer read a write up that his kids—Magin, Mike and Dan—had put together for a Father's Day tribute, which included having O'Brien stand on the Red Sox dugout while his image was projected on the large centerfield screen.

John said it was "an unbelievable experience, and one that I will never forget, and I wish every veteran could have been in my shoes because the Father's Day tribute done by my children was really for those veterans, as well."

O'Brien told the me last weekend that "no one in the crowd knew me, except for my family." He said the country has come a long way and now really embraces our veterans, guardsmen, and reservists.

When O'Brien was asked to stand and be recognized on Father's Day as a decorated veteran from Orford, New Hampshire, the announcer told the 38,000 fans: "In 1967, John O'Brien enlisted in the United States Army and served as a platoon leader and company commander with the combat engineers in Vietnam. During his 11 months of active duty there, he earned two Purple Hearts and a Bronze Star, among other military decorations and awards.

"After returning home, he continued his military service in the Air National Guard, retiring 20 years later in 1990 with the rank of Lieutenant Colonel. As commander of the 157th Civil Engineering Squadron at Pease Air Force Base in Portsmouth, New Hampshire, he was awarded the Meritorious Service Medal and the Air Force Commendation Medal.

"To this day, John has a passionate commitment to all veterans and to his local community of Orford, where he regularly coordinates veterans' recognition ceremonies. He also advocates to local newspapers on behalf of veterans for recognition of their service."

John said that after a newspaper write up (written by his children) was read by the baseball announcer at Fenway Park, there was a long standing ovation and applause from the fans which he said was for all veterans and proof "that our sacrifices and our service are truly appreciated." The Sox, by the way, came from behind and won one of the most exciting games of the year, 14 to 10.

Sue Martin of Bradford informed me of the Father's Day event at Fenway Park and the tribute to John O'Brien and other veterans. Sue and her husband, Larry Martin, know John O'Brien well as a good guy and an excellent forester, and also as an outstanding veterans' advocate no matter where those veterans may be.

I've known John for many years. He is an outstanding individual and I know him to be extremely modest and never one to want a spotlight shining on him. He was certainly deflecting that spotlight to make sure it was also shown on others.

The crowd reaction that night at Fenway Park was unbelievable. He said that cheering lasted from the end of one inning to the beginning of the next inning. "There are no words to describe the thrill of that moment. I was humbled to receive such an honor and sincerely wish it could've been shared with all veterans and members of our Armed Forces. They need to know that our country truly appreciates their service and sacrifices."

The photographs of John appearing on the big screen were sent to me by his children. I have never met his children, nor did I know anything about the Fenway Park honors. When I opened the attachments with the photographs, I saw the outdoor billboard. It was a sports story and the guy on this green looked remarkably like my friend John O'Brien of Orford.

I looked little closer and I thought that I do believe that may be John O'Brien of Orford. And when I read the description on the side of the billboard noting that "the Red Sox offer a hats off to hero, retired Lieutenant Colonel John A. O'Brien of Orford, New Hampshire," I knew it was he.

I like having good people recognized for their deeds and for what they stand for. The Red Sox spotlight for O'Brien was one of the most creative ways to say thank you to a dad I can imagine. Magin, Mike and Dan should know that this area also appreciates veterans like their dad, who served their country, came home and settled down to life as a civilian. Sometimes it's difficult to cast aside those days gone by.

John O'Brien has been a good soldier, citizen and friend of area veterans no matter where or when they served.

So, a thank you to Sue Martin for the information. Thank you, also, to John O'Brien's children for sharing this great story with me, and thank you, John, for your friendship, your courage and your support of veterans everywhere.

FORMER HAVERHILL POLICE CHIEF STEVE SAVAGE REMEMBERED

(2014)

My former Police chief was a friend and fellow veteran. He served in Vietnam as a US Air Force dog handler.

Back in 1986, Haverhill threw one of the biggest parties it had ever known to say "goodbye" to a respected police chief many people liked and appreciated. He was a Claremont boy, went to school there, graduated from Stevens High School, then joined the US Air Force and went to be a part of the Vietnam War as a security dog handler.

Steve Savage came back alive, joined the Baltimore Police Department as a drug task force officer, served at the Newport Police Department for a couple of years, then came to Haverhill as police chief in 1977. At the time, the police department was inside the old courthouse building in Woodsville, where all other town and school operations were housed.

Our Marvin clan moved to Haverhill in 1978—a year after Steve Savage arrived—and somehow, shortly after that, Chief Savage found out I had previously been part of the Kingston, Massachusetts Police Department, plus a member of the 772 MP Company Special Reaction Team of the Massachusetts National Guard and had served before that as a US Marine.

He and a buddy of his, former Sherriff of Suffolk County, Massachusetts, Roger Wells of North Haverhill, arrived at the dooryard of our old farmhouse in Haverhill one day to say "Hello," and before they left two hours later, had secured from me a promise that I would visit the Haverhill Police Department to see if I might apply there as a cruiser operator on a part-time basis. I made that visit a short time later and it began a long friendship with Steve Savage. At one time in 1979, Polly and I and our sons Bernie and Spencer were all part of HPD: Polly was secretary and dispatcher, I was a cruiser operator and young sons Bernie and Spencer were cadet members of the department. Something must have clicked there, because I remained with the department 12 years, Bernie later went into professional firefighting and Spencer entered full-time police work, both boys making those emergency services their life careers.

Three years ago, Steve was diagnosed with kidney cancer and last week he died. We had remained friends, even though he left HPD in 1986 to become the chief of Plaistow Police Department, where he remained until his recent death. Spencer and I traveled to Plaistow to pay final respects to our friend and former boss. He was a good chief and the tributes paid him by members of his department and some of his long-time friends were quite moving. All those stories of humorous mannerisms displayed by Steve were fun to recall, but quite sad to remember.

Our family knew him well. We all raised turkeys together at our place in Haverhill. During the same period, I had to face him with the news that a 12-by-12–inch timber had pierced and totally flattened his mobile police command trailer that was stored for the winter in our barn. That huge barn went down one dark and blowy December night, the animals inside were spared, but the department trailer was a goner. Steve took the news reasonably well and never stored another thing with the Marvins.

Then there was the time the department gang was at our house one Saturday helping clean up the destroyed barn. Steve had parked his international truck on the lawn with the other vehicles. Spencer, getting even with the chief for an earlier trick he had played on him, drew a large "For Sale, $50.00" sign and placed it on the chief's windshield. It was not long before someone came by, inquired to me about the truck for sale for $50.00 and I directed him to the "fella on the ladder, right over there."

Spencer managed to run faster than the chief that day, but we all had a good laugh, even Steve. Oh, yes, then there was the time we took the chief to Bath while we fished, and he watched. He was not a fisherman, but we kept urging him to give it a try. He refused on several occasions, just as well, too, for we had earlier set up a trap. We had asked a Fish and Game Department Conservation Officer to keep an eye on our group (unobserved) and if, indeed, Steve did manage to take the fishing rod (as we had begged him to do) into his unlicensed hand, the trap would be sprung, much to our delight. But Steve smelled a rat and would not handle the fishing rod. Gad Zooks! Foiled again!

Steve was a true Godfather of the town. He ordered community policing and his officers walked many miles throughout the Woodsville Village area in the evenings. We would talk to residents and stop in at businesses to chat with owners and customers. We consistently visited the schools and sat down for lunch with students. The kids and teachers really liked that. The officers did, too.

Steve would counsel battered women, people down on their luck, a kid who was having problems in school. They would flock to his office to seek his opinions and guidance. He was a mentor to many, and a consistent comment Spencer and I heard while at his services and at the cemetery was that he was a respected mentor. The Town of Plaistow loved Steve Savage and were genuinely sad about is death.

Steve's pallbearers were selected from the ranks of his town police and fire departments, plus his personal friends. One of those pallbearers was Jay Holden of Woodsville, who remained a pal of Steve's throughout the 28 years the chief was at the helm of the Plaistow Police Department.

It was a sad journey to Plaistow to be with Chief Savage that final day, but one high point was the many great Steve Savage stories told by his friends and fellow police officers. We knew and loved Steve Savage because he was a great department leader, courageous in action, fair and concerned for the safety of all the town's residents.

NURSE ANESTHETIST AND VIETNAM VETERAN JACK NEARY REMEMBERED

(2019)

Author Susan O'Neill wrote about a friend of mine in her new book. I was amazed to see his name, as Jack always had little to say about is role in the Vietnam War.

How surprised I was to see the name of former Groton, Vermont, resident, the late Jack Neary, appear in a book that I had been assigned to read with a group I'm a member of at the Veterans Administration Hospital in White River Junction.

One of my pleasures of life living in the North Country being a veteran is to have a close affiliation with the VA Hospital and some of its programs there. The Combat Veterans Book Group meets each fall and winter on an every-other-week basis. Each year our members (there are about 15) are presented with a list of four books to read and discuss during the four months the group meets. There is always a lot of group participation relative to any of the books we've read, as they all include a wide range of military subjects.

The intention of the program is to provide an opportunity for veterans to connect with other veterans, build relationships, read insightful material and share experiences. During every session, we reflect, share ideas, ask a lot of questions and receive a lot of answers about what I can say is valued and important discussion among all the group members.

The group is led by retired history professor and Vietnam veteran Michael Heaney, and retired Army Nurse and VA employee Kate Van

Cottage Hospital Nurse Anesthetist Jack Neary of Groton, Vermont. Neary is shown here with a new compact disc presented to him by the Bath, New Hampshire, music group The Rocking Chairs after the celebrated group created a song, "*Magic Jack,*" in his honor. The song gave praise to Jack's magical powers for healing bodily aches and pains. Jack, a Vietnam War veteran, was also mentioned in the popular book *Don't Mean Nothing* by author and fellow Vietnam War veteran Susan O'Neill. Neary provided O'Neill, also a nurse in Vietnam, with technical background assistance for her writing about Neary's combat specialty. Neary died in 2009. Image credit: *The Bridge Weekly*, Bernie Marvin.

Arman. Both play an important role with our group of veterans who have served in combat.

One of the four books we've been assigned this year is *Don't Mean Nothing*, a book of short stories of Vietnam by Susan O'Neill, a New York resident. She spent a year as an Army nurse in Vietnam during the war. This was her first book and it was published by Serving House Books of New Jersey. In her book, author O'Neill explained that she used Jack Neary as a reference for a fictional nurse anesthetist she wrote about.

Jack was a popular figure around Cottage Hospital in Woodsville, New Hampshire, and I had the opportunity to know him while I was doing some public relations work there at the time. Jack had been employed there as director of the anesthesia department in 1985 and worked at the hospital for over 23 years.

I remember Jack when he started his pain clinic at the hospital, and he became well known in the area as the fellow who could relieve a person's pain. He was well known in pain management circles throughout New England and won many awards because of his knowledge and dedication to caring for his patients.

Jack is probably one of the few pain clinic professionals who ever had a song written about his good work that made people feel better. During the time he was at Cottage Hospital, Jack Neary got to know members of the well-known musical group from nearby Bath, The Rocking Chairs, led by Mike Lusby. Seems that members of the band all had pain here and there and received considerable wise counsel and treatment from Jack Neary and his pain control program. The band members had such great success with Jack's "magic" treatment that they wrote and dedicated a song to his professional ability of making pain go away.

I remember the night the song was unveiled in 2007 by The Rocking Chairs to a thunderous crowd of loyal followers and to Jack Neary's family and friends. It was a fun night and Jack thoroughly enjoyed being the subject of a song rendered by the area's favorite rock 'n roll group. I don't recall many of the lyrics, but I do remember the title was "Magic Jack." I also remember one of the lines that repeated "Help me, help me, Magic Jack. I feel I'm having a heart attack." The group pounded out the notes and gave forth with at least four stanzas all in tribute to Jack's magic in treating patients' pain. It was quite a night dedicated to the talents of a wonderful person.

GEORGE TOMPKINS RETIRED AS A DYNAMITE BLASTER

(2015)

He told me his favorite food was Spam. Fried or raw! Smothered in ketchup. That George Tompkins, he was an awesome guy!

George Tompkins lived near Lake Tarleton in Piermont and died recently after a long fight with lung cancer. His services were last Sunday, where he was fondly remembered by a wide range of family and friends.

George was a unique individual whom my wife Polly and I met shortly after we moved to Piermont in 2006. We moved 3.9 miles south from Haverhill where we lived for 30 years, to our new log home in Piermont. Although it was a new town for us, we found people very friendly. It was not long before were meeting a lot of new friends in this small town, whose population hovers around 760.

Among the first people we were introduced to were George and Joyce Tompkins. They had come to town two years before we arrived, and during our first Christmas season in our new log home, we were invited to the Tompkins's for their annual Christmas gathering. We met many warm, welcoming people that night. It was my first contact with George Tompkins, someone I found to be an interesting guy with a lot of the same likes I had. One thing I found out was that George was a dynamite blaster during his lifetime of work.

What a lucky fellow—he blew thing up, like earthworks, for projects such as major road construction. He had his own blasting company where they lived in New Jersey prior to moving here.

I also have an interest in blasting that goes back to my Marine Corps days, when I was attached briefly to a Pioneer Company, those being the Marines who sweep for buried mines and bombs and clear paths through astonishingly dangerous areas.

As an extension of his blasting knowledge and training, George also made his own fireworks. I had never met someone who was a practicing pyrotechnical exploder, who designed, packed and launched his own personal line of fireworks. Fascinating.

At a Veterans Day gathering (George was a former member of the US Army and served a tour in the Vietnam War) we had at our house several years ago, George set off many of his home-created fireworks and it was a vivid display of glimmering colors and noise. At a later fireworks show, he launched a series of cascading emerald-green Roman Candle fireworks that was a very beautiful sight for the assembled crowd.

Our similarities did not stop there. I was also fascinated to find that he was a "Spam" man, meaning that he was brought up on ample supplies of the canned American favorite delicacy of spiced ham, Spam. Our conversations of our childhood eating habits also revealed that George Tompkins devoured, as I once did, Velveeta—that famous golden, smooth-flowing cheese substance in a jar, used by our mothers to make America's most favorite food: mac and cheese.

When George was not talking chow, he was serving his community. He was a member of the Piermont Zoning Board and was involved with testing the water quality of Lakes Armington and Tarleton. He was also part of the Lake Host Program, helping to keep invasive weed growth out of those waters. He was also a member of the Lake Tarleton Association Executive Board. The efforts of George Tompkins and others within his circle of concerned residents are responsible for the sparkling water quality we see today at Lakes Armington and Tarleton.

Throughout the years I knew George Tompkins, he would be eagerly assisting with many town projects, where both he and Joyce (among some of her town commitments were town and school moderator) would be lugging and tugging and cleaning with a host of friends, all pulling together to make the project happen successfully.

In a unique combination of service to both his community and his country, George Tompkins was a man that communities like Piermont are fortunate to have in their midst.

America, Romania, Korea and Beyond

Serving everywhere, serving everyone!

JUNE 25 MARKED 70 YEARS SINCE THE INVASION OF SOUTH KOREA IN 1950

(2020)

A North Haverhill resident who was a child of eight at the time, was in South Korea with his family on that fateful day.

"The Korean War started on Sunday, June 25, 1950. It was a brilliant, clear spring day in Seoul, but despite the cloudless sky there seemed to be a rumble of thunder to the north. It was artillery. My parents were missionaries of the Methodist Church and had brought me and my brother to Korea two years previously. On that Sunday I was eight, my brother Bill was five and we had a new brother, Ron, who was just six weeks old."

And so, started a history of the opening day of the Korean War as seen through the eyes of an eight-year-old child. His story is entitled "The First Experience of War." It was written several years ago by North Haverhill resident David Moore. David is the minister at the Warren Methodist Church and lives in North Haverhill with his family. His wife, Joanne, is a retired local schoolteacher. Their grown children, David and Vanessa Moore, attended Haverhill schools and are now living out of the area.

Presently, Lieutenant Colonel David Moore is a retired Marine Corps officer and Vietnam veteran. He served many years as the administrator at Cottage Hospital and participated for several years in veterans programs in the area.

His story of that morning in Seoul, Korea continues: "After church, we went up to my uncle's house at the Oriental Missionary Society compound on a hill overlooking Seoul. My aunt and uncle were

Reverend Edwin and Edna Kilbourne, who had just been refugees fleeing the Communists from Shanghai the year before. Uncle Ed was looking out over the city with binoculars.

"'They're putting up anti-aircraft guns in the City Hall Square,' Uncle Ed said. We boys scrambled for turn to look through the binoculars. A lone, single-engine prop plane flew over the city. We didn't know it then, but it was a Yak fighter from the North Korean Air Force which had just strafed Kimpo Airport north of the city."

David Moore's story of the opening of the Korean War, as he and his family were stationed in Seoul, describes troubles they had seen and heard during their first years in Korea. He wrote of meeting many pastors who told stories of relatives and friends who had been kidnapped or assassinated by terrorists from the north. He vividly remembers one night a photographer from the embassy came to his house and informed his parents he just photographed a murder scene of a Korean assemblyman and his entire family in their home just one block from their house. Young David Moore secretly listened from the stair landing as the man described the murder scene.

He recalls several other incidents of violence and death in the country prior to the invasion from the north. He said missionaries where targets of the terrorists, and eventually missionary compounds were guarded by Korea National Policemen. He wrote that the North Koreans controlled the hydroelectric power in the north, and every evening at dusk the electricity would be turned off and his electric train set would "whir to a halt." He did his homework by kerosene lamp and knew beyond all doubt the Communists "were the bad guys."

"On the night of June 25, 1950, the Moore family was all sound asleep when our neighbor, missionary Carl Judy, came and woke us up. 'Turn on Armed Forces radio,' he said. 'Operation highball is in effect and all American women and children are to report to the embassy with hand baggage only.'"

From there, his story describes how the children got up and got dressed, were loaded on military buses, said their goodbyes and drove off into the night. He said an armed Marine was on each bus as they fled the city. At the Han River Bridge there was a delay because South Korean army engineers were rigging the bridge to blow it up. Luckily, his bus was allowed to pass safely, but the bridge was blown later, and it was packed with fleeing Korean refugees.

David Moore of North Haverhill, New Hampshire, is the retired minister from the Warren Methodist Church and former administrator at Cottage Hospital in Woodsville, New Hampshire. He is seen here at the grave of his father, James H. Moore. David and his family were living in Seoul, South Korea, the day the Korean War began on June 25, 1950. Image credit: Moore Family photo.

David Moore continued describing his experiences as families continued their escape plan, and soon there were 700 American, British and Canadian women and children in their group. The men had been told to stay behind and surrender to the invading North

Korean People's Army. They were loaded onto a bus. There was no food to be had and young David Moore thought that "it was an adventure, and I rode atop a pile of baggage in the back of the bus."

In time, the refugees reached Inchon Harbor where they were quickly hidden from North Korean planes, which were ranging up and down the peninsula. He remembered receiving oatmeal cookies with raisins and walnuts from his mother. He had his tonsils removed just two weeks prior and he became ill from the hard cookies. "They made me lie down on a stretcher and an Army nurse examined me. She said there was no ice pack for my throat, all hospitals were now in a combat zone or had been captured. She turned away swearing."

Eventually the refugees were loaded on a Norwegian ship, with young David being carried by stretcher onto a Korean junk and ferried out to the boat where he finally arrived on deck.

He describes life aboard the ship. They were given blankets and chocolate, and the ship's galley opened a soup kitchen and the refugees were finally fed. He wrote that overhead US Air Force maintain air cover and a US Navy destroyer escorted the two freighters that were bringing the refugees to safety. After three days and two nights at sea, the freighters hove to just outside the mouth of Japan's Fukuoka Harbor.

They were quickly processed by the US Navy and housed at an Imperial Japanese Naval Hospital. "It was better than summer camp," he wrote. "There were movies 24 hours a day, the snack bar was always open, there were big meals and everything was free."

At the naval hospital, the group learned that General Douglas MacArthur had countermanded the ambassador's earlier orders for all US civilian men to surrender to the invading forces. Instead the general had sent transports planes to pick them up. His father was among those who survived.

"At the hospital, we kids could look down into the courtyard from our fourth-floor gymnasium windows and we saw US flag-draped caskets being unloaded. In the hospital corridors, we met American soldiers in pajamas with arm slings and bandages. We asked them what had happened, they said, 'I got shot over in a place called Korea.' The war had begun."

On July 27, 1953, after David Moore and his family escaped from Korea, the shooting war ended in a cease-fire. A total of more than 36,000 US military personnel and 140,000 South Korean troops were killed in action during the war.

I REMEMBER "COMMANDER JT" LEADING HIS AMERICAN LEGION HONOR GUARD

(2013)

His passing evoked other memories as well, including zoning issues at town meetings, the 111 Club, his coin-operated laundromat, his famous Sho-Case, *Camp Tuck Press and his frequent phone calls.*

It was sad news to find out that a north country institution died last Sunday morning. Julius E. Tueckhardt, Jr., was a fixture in Woodsville, an activist for many causes, the long-time Commander of the Ross–Wood American Legion Post 20, business owner and the thorn in the side of all zoning proponents everywhere. He was an enthusiastic energy machine and a special person in these parts.

"Tuck" as most called him (I called him "JT," and he always reciprocated by hailing me by a part of my last name, "Hey, Marv"), was usually on the leading edge of most contrarian issues in town, including zoning, some police budget numbers and other public matters that came across his path. He never flinched at an opportunity to use his publication, *The Sho-Case*, to tell his vast readership his opinion on any number of projects or programs happening or about to happen in Haverhill. He would launch into his critical viewpoint, explain the project, why he did or did not support it, then offer a VOTE YES or a VOTE NO position. He never minced words and he swung a lot of public opinion his way.

In a John Hancock swirl with his blunt-end Sharpie so every reader could see it, he would sign his opinion piece editorials with his sweeping signature, bold, black, and big, an act no other local paper publisher ever had the courage to do. JT did, though.

The world of puff piece journalism—white tower editorialists—filled with their own sappy brand of "taking a position" would never sign their name to an editorial, and upon someone asking who in the world would write such pointed, political, one-way trash, the shrinking editorial page Superman would only say, "The paper wrote it." JT never lived in the world of the area newspaper moguls who prohibited their names to appear on their personal opinion editorials. JT signed them—every one of them—with his definitive brand.

Probably his biggest and most successful ongoing sustained campaign was against zoning the town of Haverhill several years ago. Each time the measure would get shot down at a town meeting vote, proponents would back off and let the subject cool. Then they would come back for more. JT never disappointed them or his readers. The zoning proponents' last attempt to get a town-wide measure passed fell to a lopsided vote of about four to one, just about the margin JT said it would be.

One year he had amassed a huge petitioned effort and gathered hundreds of names to squelch some town-sponsored measure he determined not to be good for the town. The presence of JT, his petition and his large army of supporters convinced whatever board it was to not put their measure on the town meeting voting ballot that year.

Over the years of participating in a lot of parades, I got to know JT well. I found that he was not only a crusader for the "little guy and gal," but he was also a helping force for them. He was behind many giveaway programs for the less fortunate. For a small business to begin an advertising program in his *Sho-Case*, he would offer rates that were very affordable to start-ups. For many others, he just might have slipped them a little grocery money here and there as well.

JT was a US Navy veteran and he would hammer on me for spending my four years of obligated time in the Marine Corps. He would remind me that the Marine Corps was a part of the Department of the Navy and that Marines were known on his ship as "Sea-Going Bellhops." I would remind him that the last time I saw his Navy in action, they dropped us off at a foreign beachhead, promptly left and we never saw them again. On and on this would flow—we both enjoyed the humorous banter.

It has been quite a while since I visited him at "Camp Tuck," his official headquarters located at 111 Central Street in Woodsville. It would be here that the coffee pot was on and the cigarette smoke was heavy and gray as his friends gathered to review the promises of a new day. JT would be at the helm, carefully reviewing his plan to look at a proposal a Haverhill board or commission was thinking of adopting. If he approved, it would be supported, if he did not approve, he would launch a program to either slow it down or kill it off.

That was JT, a real influence a community.

BEHIND EVERY GOOD VFW POST, THERE IS A LADIES' AUXULIARY

(2014)

Behind every good VFW member, there is a VFW Auxiliary member, ready to serve, ready to help!

The Veterans of Foreign Wars Post 5245 in North Haverhill was the scene of a special celebration last Sunday. The VFW Ladies' Auxiliary of the post was honored for serving the nation and its Veterans of Foreign Wars for 100 years. They are in the midst of their centennial celebration and last Sunday's observance included all the local women who have been members of that post at one time or another since it was founded and chartered back in 1948.

There is one surviving Charter Member of the Ladies' Auxiliary. She is Mary Hutchins of Haverhill and she received a special award for being a member for the past 66 years. Many other members were honored as well during a ceremony that saw VFW Ladies' Auxiliary District 2 President, Janice Sackett, present distinguished service certificates. Former VFW Post 5245 Commander Wayne Fortier read two poems written by post member Ed Ball of Warren.

Ball, a Vietnam veteran, also read two poems he had written for his family explaining the pain of war. According to Janice Sackett, the North Haverhill Post of the Ladies' Auxiliary was chartered in 1948. They met twice monthly at the Odd Fellows Hall, and their $5.00 monthly rent was split with the VFW Post. The members were always referred to as "Sisters" in the official minutes of each meeting. The meetings began at 8 PM.

Don and Barbara Stevens of Piermont, New Hampshire, when they were hailed as Parade Marshals for the Woodsville–Wells River July 4th Parade several years ago. Barbara was an active member of Post 5245 Veterans of Foreign Wars Ladies Auxiliary. That was also Don's VFW Post, where he served faithfully for decades as a respected World War II veteran of the European Theater. Image credit: *The Bridge Weekly*, Bernie Marvin.

Mary Hutchins, I am told, joined as Mary Brooks: her maiden name. She was joined at the meeting Sunday by Barbara Stevens, who has been a member for 63 years. Dot Martin has been a member for 61 years. Bertha Aremburg has been a member for 54 years. Mildred Williams has been a member for 51 years.

There were many others who have served less than 50 years, but it was an impressive reading of the roll that included the many women in the area who have joined the Auxiliary under the names of their VFW family members that included their husbands, brothers, fathers, and even under their grandfather's name. Their names on the program read like a tapestry woven of the town's history and included a membership of more than 90 names.

Also part of the program were Donna Bagley and Donna Hopkins. A surprise guest, who has appeared on stages throughout the area, appeared last Sunday to provide a brief entertainment session for guests. The appearance of Minnie Pearl, complete with a zany flower-bedecked hat, provided a laugh. Minnie has been doing her routine since 1972, she told me stage-side. She is also known around the circuit as Janice Sackett.

A luncheon was provided as part of the celebration for these gracious and dedicated ladies who serve their communities to honor the sacrifices and commitment of every man and woman who has served.

Happy 66th!!

AREA TOWNSPEOPLE WILL MISS BOB CLIFFORD AND HIS PATRIOTISM

(2010)

Bob Clifford was a master carpenter and assisted local veterans with each July 4th float they entered in the Woodsville–Wells River Parade.

The town was shocked last Sunday morning to learn of the unexpected death of Bob Clifford of North Haverhill. Bob was a loyal and hard-working resident who knew everyone in the area, had made a ton of friends and was a steadfast and honorable patriot.

I knew Bob Clifford well, worked with him on a dozen military projects and floats for the July 4th Parade and admired how quickly he would jump into our local veterans' projects, helping to complete some amazing tasks with hustle, pride and spirit. Bob was one of those guys who made you happy he was your friend and ally.

Bob was a strong supporter of the military and had served in the uniform of the New Hampshire National Guard for nearly 40 years. No matter what had to be obtained for whatever purpose, Bob Clifford could get it. He was the best supply sergeant I ever knew! If he couldn't find one, he built one.

For one July 4th Parade float that we were creating not too many years ago to honor our Vietnam War veterans, we needed to get our hands on a couple of automatic weapons—not an easy task in this society where anything that shoots faster that a cap pistol or has a handle on it or a bayonet lug is classified as an assault weapon and therefore is not suitable, I am told, for local parades.

But, our group of local veterans always prided themselves in being authentic and when we needed REAL automatic weapons in the hands of our warriors on parade to make our Vietnam statues authentic, Bob saw to it that we got REAL automatic weapons to parade with. On the morning of July 4th, in walks Bob Clifford with an M-60 machine gun and an M-16 rifle, all checked out and ready for our band of brothers to march with. I asked Bob where on earth he could come up with those items, and he said it was quite easy, but quite classified.

Those flags flying on every phone pole in North Haverhill Village—that's another one of Bob's projects, just as were countless Memorial Day flag placements in the local cemeteries. Prior to each Memorial Day, he and his grandson, Jacob Clifford, would place up to 800 American flags on veterans' graves throughout the town. He turned that project into a school exercise by inviting classes from the Haverhill Cooperative Middle School to assist. He told me during one day in the Center Haverhill Cemetery that this is how kids learn, by having them placing a flag at a veteran's tombstone.

There is so much more to Bob Clifford and his various projects throughout the town that included even more than his devotion to the country and its military. And now comes the time for the town to pay Bob Clifford back for a portion for his dedication to Haverhill. His old brick armory that he served in for so many years as an enlisted man while serving in the New Hampshire National Guard needs to be named in a fitting manner. That building on Route 135 in Woodsville, the National Guard Armory, recently purchased by the Town of Haverhill, should be marked with a name that evokes respect, honor, pride and tradition, something Bob always stood for. What a fitting way to honor the name and deeds of Robert E. Clifford.

Thank you, Bob for your devoted friendship over the years and thank you for your valued assistance with every float and project our group of veterans ever created. Semper Fidelis from your band of brothers and sisters who mourn your passing. We will all cherish attending future events at the Robert E. Clifford Memorial Building.

Author's Note: The old armory referred to above has been named by the Town of Haverhill as the Robert E. Clifford Memorial Building.

TOM GILLEN WROTE THIS STORY ON SOME OF HIS UNDERSEA ADVENTURES

(2020)

My friend Tom Gillen from Haverhill Corner wrote a note telling me how he mentioned to his wife, Paula, that the isolation they were in during the world pandemic brought on with COVID-19 brought back old memories and feelings of his time in submarines in the 1960s. She suggested he write down those memories, so that others might enjoy reading them. Tom wrote them down. I told him his story was terrific and I was pleased to include it in this book of veterans' adventures.

LIKE A LONG PATROL

By Tom Gillen

When the pandemic lockdown started around March 17, 2020, I didn't think much about it other than we'd be staying home a lot and would have to be careful when we did have to go out for groceries. My wife and I are retired and tend to spend more time around the house rather than going out all the time, so I figured, "OK, we can deal with it." We always seem to keep ourselves busy with various hobbies and projects around the house. As we got more into the lockdown, we noticed that it was a bit hard not at least having the option to say, "Let's go to the store," or drive here or there on a whim if we wanted. As we progressed, memories and feelings from a long time ago started to come to mind for me.

In the 1960s I was a young man in the Navy Submarine service. I was stationed on an early nuclear submarine, the USS *Snook* (SSN

U.S. Navy FTG3(SS) Petty Officer Third Class Tom Gellen, Fire Control Technician of Haverhill Corner, New Hampshire, in the forward torpedo room of the *USS Snook* (SSN-592) on Westpac in late 1969 in Japan. While on Westpac, Gellen said they carried a full war load of torpedoes, including the Mk37, Mk 14, Mk 16, Mk 48 and a classified unit. Image credit: Gellen Family photo.

592). Our main limitation on how long we could stay at sea was pretty much based on our food supply. I remember well our typical western Pacific deployments—or as they were known, WESTPAC. On a typical WESTPAC we were away for about 7 or 8 months, and of that time we were underwater for about 6 months. During 1966, Snook steamed for 35,000 miles, of which 34,000 were submerged. That was a lot of time isolated, underwater and no with choice about it. When we left port, the minute we had enough water under us we submerged, and we didn't surface until coming back into port when our keel was almost scraping the bottom.

During our patrols, the Navy knew the area where we were supposed to be patrolling but had no idea where we actually were, and no contact with us other than scheduled broadcasts from them that they assumed we received. We transmitted absolutely nothing and were on quiet patrol all the time. If we had trouble we were on our own and the Navy would have no idea we were in trouble until we didn't show back up at the end of our patrol when we were due back in port.

Where we were on patrol, we could not surface for anything since it would likely cause a huge incident, so we were on our own. This was during the Cold War and the Russian trawlers were active and really wanted to dissuade us from where we were patrolling, and also were trying hard to track us. Our typical routine while on WESTPAC was a 60- to 70-day patrol, and then a week or so in some port for stores, liberty and repairs. And then we'd do it all over again.

During my time on Snook, we left for a WESTPAC from San Diego to Hawaii, then Subic Bay in the Philippines. Then Hong Kong via Vietnam, Yokosuka Japan, Okinawa, Guam and back to San Diego via Hawaii.

With this background in mind you can see why, just now passing the current 60-day mark from the pandemic, memories from the long patrols return. Meals in particular stir up recollections. As then, now too I tend to think and plan my day based on meals like we did on patrols. Meals on the sub were very important for morale. I especially remember midnight watches when I was fairly new onboard, so my duty station was helmsman piloting the sub. During the mid-watch, sometimes the night baker would bring freshly baked bread or other goodies up to the control room for the watch standers. What a treat it was.

I will always remember those long watches. Our diving officer on some of those mid-watches was a chief torpedoman who had been on

World War II submarines and on a sub that went into Tokyo harbor. His tales were right out of all the submarine movies you ever watched but he actually had been there. The history he told was amazing.

Like I mentioned, meals were not just a meal—they were much more. It was relief from the boredom. It was catching up with your shipmates and playing cards or watching a movie. It was a small amount of down time from the 6 hours on and 6 hours off of watch to decompress a little—to not pay attention to what was happening on the patrol.

I remember one time when a new commissary man who had never provisioned a sub under-packed for a patrol, even with the usual Navy documents to help with planning. Toward the end of patrol we were running low on food. To make matters worse, we received orders via one of our scheduled receive-only broadcasts to remain on station for another 2 weeks.

There was nothing we could do. By the end of the patrol we were down to Spam, cans of dehydrated cottage cheese and instant mashed potatoes. The cooks tried to make things seem better by calling Spam at breakfast "grilled," dinner was "baked," and so forth. The potatoes were called "fried" at breakfast, "roasted" at noon and "snowflake" at dinner, but they were all the exact same. Morale at the end of that patrol was not the best. To this day I can't even think of eating Spam and feel much the same about instant mashed potatoes.

So here I sit on May 17, 2020, like I just finished a patrol and now will get ready to do it all over again into at least June or July, with all the memories and feelings from a long time ago returning. My wife and I will do this routine for however many more months we have to so we protect others and remain safe ourselves from the virus. The big difference is that we can, every so often, carefully go to the market for supplies or do curbside pickup from Walmart or have Amazon ship it in. We have access to unlimited books, movies and other content from the internet. I have much more space available than I did on the sub, and have access to the outside of the house and am able to roam around the garden in the fresh air and sunlight.

Not bad compared to the past "long patrols" in the '60s that I was on. And, please remember that the same things are still going on now for the men in the submarine fleet and the other Navy sailors on ships and soldiers on the ground being isolated and being issued Meals Ready to Eat for many days and months at a time. I think of way back then, and what our troops are doing today, or what people in cities like New York are going through now with COVID-19, and I figure, "I've got this, no problem."

PHOTOJOURNALIST DICKEY CHAPELLE WAS WITH CASTRO WHEN HE MARCHED INTO HAVANA

(2016)

I had earlier served with Dickey Chapelle on another of her war assignments in Beirut, Lebanon. Her newest adventure was quite different, with the Castro brothers and Che.

The death of former Cuban Revolutionary President Fidel Castro this year brought me back to a day in 1959 when I was stationed in Arlington, Virginia. In early May that year, I was invited by combat photographer Dickey Chapelle to watch her photo presentation of an event she participated in: the entry into Havana, Cuba by the leader of the famed 26th of July Movement, Fidel Castro, and his revolutionary army.

Dickey told me of Castro, a Communist and revolutionary mountain fighter, who overcame big odds with his small rag-tag army to overthrow the regime of authoritarian strong man, Fulgencio Batista. From then on, and until last week when Castro died, the island of Cuba had been strictly controlled by Castro or, in the last few years, by the regime presently in place led by Castro's brother, Raul.

Some of the extreme and dangerous trade barriers in place between Cuba and the United States have been relaxed a bit, but Cuba remains today a totalitarian state, just as it was back in 1959 when Castro and his revolutionaries took over.

Dickey Chapelle was a civilian photographer whom I met during the invasion of Lebanon in the Middle East. She was assigned to various magazines, such as *Readers Digest*, *National Geographic* and others to photograph the action as she accompanied our US Marine units in country.

The next time I met Dickey was when she visited my Marine Base Henderson Hall unit at Arlington, Virginia a year later for the purposes of showing us her exploits and her photos she shot while accompanying Castro as he fought Batista's army in the Sierra Maestre Mountains and then marched victoriously into Havana in the first week of January 1959.

From that day forward, Castro ruled the island with an iron hand, and not too long after his victorious entry into the city, he showed his full intentions as a conquering nationalist as he took over the country and every private enterprise therein.

Dickey got it all on film and it was a fascinating afternoon as she revealed the long struggle and finally Comandante Castro's overwhelming victory. She also captured photographs of other exploits of Castro and his brother Raul, and of the legendary Ernesto Che Guevara (killed in Bolivia in 1967) who called for retribution for Batista's followers in the words of "Pa-Re-Don! To the Wall!"

Executions at the wall followed, so did the Bay of Pigs Invasion in April 1961, the Cuban Missile Crisis in October 1962 and a long list of bad feelings and confrontations from then on while the Soviet Union embraced Communist Cuba, just 90 miles from the US shore.

Today, not a whole lot has changed in Cuba, although it might someday. A friend of mine from Piermont, New Hampshire, travelled to Cuba two years ago when the thaw between Cuba and the USA was underway. I asked her what it was like to travel to Cuba, as I had never been there. Her comments follow:

"Was Fidel Castro alive when I went to Cuba? Our tour director didn't know, nor did the people with whom we were allowed to talk, but one thing was certain: his footprint was on everything we saw, everything we did and every place we ate.

"In order to visit, I had to get a Cuban people-to-people visa and join an accepted tour that had a tight itinerary and little time to explore this beautiful paradise of an island. In spite of this, it remains as one of my most memorable trips. I can still picture the people whose warm smiles welcomed us everyplace we went.

"We were told that Castro's brother, Raul, was now in charge and 'that it was better than under his brother's rule,' which left us wondering how this could be so. Fidel Castro was extremely ill, hadn't been seen in months and perhaps had died, but the government wasn't ready to announce it yet.

"During one lecture, I asked how the Cubans would react when his death became a reality. With jubilation? Sorrow? 'I will cry for days,' said one speaker who had spent the past hour telling us how every iota of their impoverished existence was government controlled.

"Perhaps the most startling moment happened when touring The Bay of Pigs. The adversarial feelings between US President John F. Kennedy and Fidel Castro were well known, although I didn't know the CIA had tried numerous times to assassinate Castro. No matter how ingenious, each attempted plan failed. But this was the jolt: our tour director told us Fidel Castro advised his colleagues at the time to tune their radio to a Dallas station at 11 AM on that fateful day that President Kennedy was assassinated on that November day in 1963."

Many Americans still believe that Fidel Castro and his Communist partners in Havana and Moscow planned the assassination.

I never saw photographer Dickey Chapelle again after her photo show. She was later killed in action in Vietnam while on patrol with the Marines. She was not a fan of the Castro brothers and told me that "Che," as he was known, was also downright dangerous. She said the Cuban people were warm and friendly and did not know what they were getting in for when they thought the Castro boys were to be their future saviors.

FORMER HAVERHILL RESIDENT TOM ESTILL RECALLS HIS CONVERSATION

(2016)

Tom remembers a conversation he had with Mrs. McAuliffe just prior to her death. They were both part of the 11,000 teachers who tried out for the program. Christa was selected for the ill-fated project.

The date of January 28, 1986 remains a sad day for many in the Granite State who had crossed paths with a Concord, New Hampshire, social studies teacher, Christa McAuliffe. Just over a minute into the flight on that day, the spacecraft *Challenger* blew up, killing all seven astronauts aboard.

There was considerable confusion on the ground, as friends, students and relatives of the seven astronauts watched in horror after Mission Control finally announced after the craft disappeared into an orange ball of flame and debris: "We have a report from the flight dynamics officer that the vehicle has exploded."

During the flight, Mrs. McAuliffe was to broadcast two lessons from space to students around the nation. She was a schoolteacher and the mother of two young children, Caroline and Scott. The space program she was a part of was known as the Teacher in Space Project, and was announced by President Ronald Reagan two years earlier.

The program was to help make science, technology, engineering and mathematics more important to students. After the inflight explosion and deaths of the entire crew, the National Air and Space Administration (NASA) cancelled the program. They replaced the Teacher in Space Project two years later with the Educator Astronaut

Program. The first Educator Astronaut was Christa McAuliffe's backup for the doomed *Challenger* flight, Barbara Morgan, who was launched from Earth aboard the space shuttle *Endeavor* in August 2007.

I remember during the turmoil after the *Challenger* explosion, a friend and Oxbow High School science teacher Tom Estill, a neighbor of mine in Haverhill, had told me all about his experiences trying out for the Teacher in Space Project. Although he missed being the honored first Teacher in Space, he was proud to have been a part of the program.

I recall how devastated Tom was when the *Challenger* accident occurred. Last week I wrote to Tom about the accident and the following is a note I received this week about his feelings that day so long ago:

> I still remember so vividly that sad January day in 1986. The Oxbow High School students gathered around the TV sets in the school library, the clapping and cheers as it successfully launched, followed shortly thereafter by bewildered looks, and then shock, tears and disbelief as reality slowly set in.
>
> I was blessed later in my life to have my dream come true of someday working for NASA and having the opportunity to meet and visit with Christa's backup, Barbara Morgan. We were dreamers, and those who dare to dream, dare to do.
>
> This week, as I lead a group of Vermont students, in the first time ever for students from that State to visit LIVE with the Space Station astronauts as they fly overhead, I'll be telling the story of the *Challenger* crew, and how our space program inspired people like Christa McAuliffe to hold onto and work towards their

> dreams, never give up and have the courage to Boldly Go Where No One Has Gone Before.

Also notable was his post-script:

> P.S. I think of Haverhill often, and miss my friends there very much. The memories of my life there will forever hold a special place in my heart.

That is a very powerful note from Tom Estill, still teaching and still involved with NASA and its youth space program.

Another person who was part of the life of Concord school teacher Christa McAuliffe was former Grafton County Attorney Rick St. Hilaire. I had come to know Rick during my travels in the area as a news writer during those days, and he was an interesting fellow to interview and to be with. One day he revealed to me how Christa McAuliffe was an important part of his young life as he was growing up in Concord.

I asked Rick to tell me what he remembered about that awful day 30 years ago when school students who knew Mrs. McAuliffe suddenly realized that the *Challenger* space vehicle had blown up and all aboard had perished. Rick's letter follows:

> Mrs. McAuliffe was my supervisor for an independent study project when I interned at the New Hampshire House. She was also the Concord High faculty supervisor for YMCA Youth and Government program … Had she made it into orbit, I was one of the six students chosen (3 from Concord High and 3 from the

school where her backup Barbara Morgan taught) to participate in the "classroom in space."

Mrs. McAuliffe always had a smile on her face. She was a fixture in the social studies department on the third floor of Concord High, so I remember being surprised to see her one day as I was walking down the first-floor corridor after she had been absent because of the Teacher in Space Program. We talked in the hallway. I remember us talking about her weightlessness training for the shuttle flight. You could tell she was very excited about going into space. That was my last conversation with her.

While the *Challenger* disaster is remembered as a national tragedy, for those of us who knew Mrs. McAuliffe, it is still felt as a personal loss. The most important thing to remember, however, is that she inspired many of my classmates and others around the US to enter the teaching profession. That is her lasting legacy.

So here we have the reactions from two people who were associated with Christa McAuliffe 30 years ago—a sad day for both of them.

Another interesting contact I had with Teacher in Space devastation from that fateful event of January 28, 1986, was a telephone call I received in March of the same year from a Woodsville resident, Mary Dupuis, who lived on Oak Hill Street. A charming lady with short white hair and a soft voice, Mary invited me into her home to show me two photos she had taken of the space vehicle *Challenger* lift off on the early morning of January 28, 1986, only a few months earlier.

She told me she traveled to the space launch area at Cape Canaveral in Florida while there on vacation to watch the historic flight and took a few photos of the event. She said I might want to use one of them in a newspaper I was writing for at the time, especially the photo that clearly showed the explosion and the crazily corkscrewing parts of the vehicle as they scattered into the frosty early morning sky.

Mrs. Dupuis had perfectly captured the tragedy that morning. I never got to use the photo and I never saw Mrs. Dupuis after our initial meeting. Interestingly, she had captured the rapidly accelerating space vehicle at the exact moment of explosion and when it came apart in midair.

It was and still remains a sad day for many of us.

ARMY TANKER CHASE MILLER DESCRIBED HIS RECENT TOUR OF ROMANIA

(2018)

This young soldier spoke frankly with his friends and peers in the classroom. He told them exactly what it was like to be in a foreign country in a US tank and be under scrutiny by the nearby Soviet Army.

Chase Miller, a 2016 graduate of Woodsville High School, returned to class in his school recently to tell a few inside stories on his basic training at Fort Benning, Georgia, and his recent training exercises in Romania.

Two years ago, PFC Miller sat in that same class taught by Robert Scianna and, as he said last week, he knew he wanted to join the military because he felt it was something he had wanted to do since he was a little kid. He did that feat of joining up in the regular, full-time Army (along with a friend of his, Jacob Clifford of North Haverhill, also a US Army Tanker), and from what I saw and heard of PFC Miller in class last week, he has been taught well, knows his role in the Army as a Private First Class and folks can look for him to excel in his role as an Army Tanker.

He told a good story, continually narrating clearly and distinctly his views and observations along the way from his transformation in life as a civilian to a trained member of his Brigade Combat Team, part of the 4th Infantry Division and stationed in Fort Carson, Colorado.

He told students some of the pains of basic training and how important it is to work together with the rest of his team members. In no time, he said, he was sent to Europe to participate in a multinational military exercise. He said his unit's mission there was to strengthen local forces who are underpowered. He said those Eastern Baltic countries included Romania, Lithuania, Estonia, Bosnia and other places in the region. He noted that Russian forces were just miles away when American troops and tanks were training in the region.

PFC Miller explained some of the comparisons of Russian versus American tanks and the shortened spans of human life when engaged in tank combat. To better show his work inside and outside of his group of M1A2 Abrams tanks, he wore a GoPro video camera during part of his stint with the tank training and showed the class exactly how it was to drop down through the hatch and enter the inside world of a tanker, complete with vivid color, living sound and a spectacular view through his own trained eyes. Right there on the screen located in a Woodsville High School classroom, students in the military history class were treated to actual video showing them just what was happening inside the Army tank as it rumbled through the Romanian countryside.

You could hear the high-pitched whining of the revved-up engine, the associated noises and the dangerous, but interesting, assignment PFC Miller really has, considering it was not that long ago that he was helping his dad in his Oliverian Automotive business in Pike, New Hampshire. Now he was deep in the Baltic Region of the world surrounded by the military forces of Russia, who had brought along a whole lot more tanks into the landscape than the forces the USA had assembled by a long shot—after all, they were operating at Russia's back door.

PFC Miller, with knowledge and feeling, described how the 72-ton iron monster was transformed from a sleeping giant into a motivated behemoth machine, complete with swallowing many gallons of gas per mile (not miles per gallon, he reminded the class). With the GoPro video displaying it all, it was hard to hear PFC Miller's voice above the roar of the tank's motor.

At one point that during the deployment to Romania, he was inside the tank for a total of 14 days. That meant no trips outside to stretch, and no personal trips to see what was happening outside. That was his primary home for two weeks.

What the class saw that day from PFC Miller was a total personal approach showing his tank and its interior through a very well-done descriptive review of the machine, as well as its equipment and what it is capable of doing. The session could not have been more professionally delivered by a senior sergeant with many years of service in tanks and associated armored vehicles.

Chase Miller has been working around and training with tanks for a little over a year. He knows how important the job is. He has traveled to Germany and Romania and beyond in this short time between his fifth-row seat, two from the back position in Mr. Scianna's military history class not that long ago.

PFC Miller is proud of what he does. His next assignment could be for his unit to go anywhere in the world, for any purpose and at any time. He realizes he is living in a dangerous environment where a change-of-assignment may come in a matter of hours.

He said he is proud of what he does, and from what I saw of PFC Miller's presentation at Woodsville High School, he certainly has a good outlook, a mature presentation and the profile of someone who will be a winner in the US Army and later at life.

10th MOUNTAIN DIVISION MEMORIAL IN LANDAFF SET FOR JULY 22nd

(2017)

A special annual memorial program will be coming to Landaff.

This will be at the newly relocated 10th Mountain Division World War II Veterans Memorial Garden that was formerly located in Lancaster. The new home for the memorial garden, on land owned by Lloyd and Joanne Donnellan of Millbrook Road, was given to the 10th Mountain Division Association so that the group of World War II veterans could still commemorate the lives of those veterans who fought and died in the mountains of Italy towards the end of World War II in 1945.

The original Memorial Garden was established in Lancaster, New Hampshire, on land owned by the Warren Bartlett family and was started 19 years ago. Every year since, a memorial service has been held at the garden in July, just as it will be held this year at the new location owned by the Donnellan family. After the Bartlett property was sold, the new owners decided they did not want the memorial garden located there, and this dilemma came to the attention of the Donnellans, who took immediate action to donate a portion of their land in Landaff, where last week finishing touches were put on the new 10th Mountain Division Memorial Garden.

Lloyd and Joanne Donnellan told me when I visited the very impressive site, which includes a large field of crosses and American flags, that there will be a special service there at the site on Saturday,

U.S. Coast Guard veteran and longtime merchant seaman Lloyd Donnellan of Landaff, New Hampshire, has created a memorial park on property in Landaff owned by him and his wife, Joanne. The serene brookside park is dedicated to the memory of New England members of the 10th Mountain Division, famed ski troops dating back to World War II. The Donnellans hold an annual Memorial Service at the site each summer, inviting surviving members, plus present 10th Mountain Division troops who have served in Afghanistan and Iraq and other countries involved in the War on Terrorism. Image credit: *The Bridge Weekly*, Bernie Marvin.

July 22nd, and will feature a military honor guard, special songs, a poem and some brief words by a special guest.

This memorial garden is dedicated to the veterans and their families of the 10th Mountain Division, which was a national mountain spec-ialist unit formed during World War II that fought in Italian mount-ains. The memorial garden in Landaff presently has 102 crosses with the names of New Englanders who fought and died with that unit.

Lloyd and Joanne Donn-ellan came to the area from Maine two years ago. Lloyd has a dog grooming business and Joanne is a nurse at the Grafton County Nursing Home. They're both involved with many projects in the area and are spirited patriots when it comes to commemorating the lives and the heroics of the 10th Mountain Division. Joanne's dad, Edward Crist, was a member of the 10th Mountain Division and saw combat with the division in Italy during World War II.

They have a large web of friends who are members of this organization and it is expected that many of them will be at the newly constructed memorial garden site on July 22nd this year.

They told me the public is invited to the service that begins at 11 AM, where visitors will get to view this sacred field of crosses with the names of deceased veterans on each one. It is a very impressive site and it's good to know that upon the near demise of the Lancaster Memorial Garden that this Landaff family stepped into the situation and told the organizers that they would be happy to host the garden on their land.

Lloyd told me that many, many volunteers and friends have jumped onto this important project and the new Memorial Garden will be ready for all to see and will be ready for the 19th annual memorial service that so appropriately pays tribute to this historic 10th Mountain Division veterans.

To update this story on the 10th Mountain Division Memorial Garden, I have included my news story written in July 2020 and published in The Bridge Weekly newspaper. Note the new name of the garden to reflect the original founders prior to the garden being relocated to Landaff, also the increased number of memorial crosses reflecting the passing of New England 10th Mountain Division veterans.

I have also included the entire narrative written by Pastor Mal Kircher of the Piermont Congregational Church. He has participated in each memorial service and has delivered eloquent tributes to the heroic division at each service. The 2020 update follows with Pastor Mal Kircher's tribute in its entirety.

10TH MOUNTAIN DIVISION HOLDS MEMORIAL SERVICE IN LANDAFF

(2020)

Hot weather once again greeted visitors and military units who participated in the twenty second 10th Mountain Division Memorial service last Saturday, July 18, 2020.

The new Bartlett–Crist 10th Mountain Memorial Garden was built on land owned by Lloyd and Joanne Donnellan of Westend Road, just off Route 302. This is the third year of the memorial service at that location, after the memorial was moved from a location in Lancaster to the impressive new site bordering the Mill Brook.

Units from the North Haverhill Veterans of Foreign Wars Post 5245 and the Ross–Wood American Legion participated in the flag raising and Taps ceremonies in memory of the 10th Mountain Division troops formed in New Hampshire in 1943 and received mountain training for their future assignments in the mountain range warfare of World War II.

When the Memorial Garden was first constructed in 1997 in Lancaster on land of one of the division's veterans, Warren Bartlett, it held a total of four crosses. Upon Bartlett's death and the sale of the property, the memorial was moved to the Donnellan's property in Landaff. The memorial garden now features 124 named crosses, each representing a departed New England member of the famed division. They were designed and installed at the site, which also includes a flagpole just above the array of white crosses with black lettering.

After the Bartlett property in Lancaster was sold, the new owner asked for the memorial garden to be relocated. That request was quickly honored by the Donnellan couple, as Joanne's father, Ed Crist, was a veteran of the division.

The Memorial Garden now includes the names of both Bartlett and Crist to honor both men's service to their country. Their vision for a future memorial garden that commemorates the Division's service—not only during World War II, but for the continuing sacrifices of today's 10th Mountain Division with combat assignments in both Iraq and Afghanistan—has also been honored.

The service was led once again by Pastor Mal Kircher of the Piermont Congregational Church.

FINDING OUR WAY HOME

By Pastor Mal Kircher

Hebrews 11:8–10, 13–16

[8] *By faith Abraham, when called to go to a place he would later receive as his inheritance, obeyed and went, even though he did not know where he was going.* [9] *By faith he made his home in the promised land like a stranger in a foreign country; he lived in tents, as did Isaac and Jacob, who were heirs with him of the same promise.* [10] *For he was looking forward to the city with foundations, whose architect and builder is God...*

[13] *All these people were still living by faith when they died. They did not receive the things promised; they only saw them and*

welcomed them from a distance, admitting that they were foreigners and strangers on earth. [14] *People who say such things show that they are looking for a country of their own.* [15] *If they had been thinking of the country they had left, they would have had opportunity to return.* [16] *Instead, they were longing for a better country—a heavenly one. Therefore God is not ashamed to be called their God, for he has prepared a city for them.*

The word "*home*" is one that captures our imagination. It is a word that has great power, that echoes in our souls, and that rouses deep longings.

Whether we live in a palace or a cabin, it's not the structure itself that's important to us, it's what that word "*home*" represents. It symbolizes that place where we find quietness, rest, peace, well-being and safety. It is a place that is comfortably familiar to us. "*Home*" speaks of shelter and support. It is a refuge—a place to which we can retreat so that we can recharge our batteries, a place where we're surrounded by those we love and by those who love us, and it's a place where we are known, and where we have a sense of belonging.

The year 2020 is the 50th anniversary of *Apollo 13*, which launched from Cape Kennedy on April 11, 1970, and safely splashed down in the South Pacific 6 days later on April 17th. What should have been the United States' third moon landing turned into a rescue mission when, on the second day of the flight, the number 2 oxygen tank blew up in the service module.

Twenty-twenty also marks the 25th anniversary of the movie *Apollo 13*, starring Tom Hanks as mission commander Jim Lovell.

In an interview made during the filming of the movie, Tom Hanks said, "There's something about the story of getting back home, which is one of the seven great stories of literature: how do you get back home? And that's what this is."

In the movie, as *Apollo 13* passes around the back side of the moon, Fred Haise and Jack Swigert are distractedly looking out the porthole in awe struck wonder at the moon's surface—just 139 nautical miles away—while Jim Lovell works around them. Finally, Jim steps back, pauses for a moment and "in a voice deliberately too loud for the tiny cockpit," says: "Gentlemen, what are your intentions?... I'd like to go home."

And when told that the networks—who didn't care about the mission when it was just about getting to the moon—want to set up transmitters on her lawn now that it has caught the world's attention, Marilyn Lovell snaps, "No, Henry! Those people don't put one piece of equipment on my lawn. If they have a problem with that, they can take it up with my husband. He'll be HOME…on FRIDAY!"

In a very real sense, World War II was about home. Stalin was fighting to save the Motherland from a foreign invader. Even the megalomaniac Adolph Hitler was supposedly fighting for the Fatherland, and for *Lebensraum*—for "living space." The men of the 10th Mountain Division—your husbands, fathers, and grandfathers—who fought their battles 75 years ago this year, were also fighting for home. They were fighting to protect the parents, sweethearts, wives, and children that they had left behind. They went to war to preserve a way of life—ballgames, Saturday afternoon matinees and cookouts in the backyard. They fought for an ideal—the self-evident truths that "all men are created equal, that they are endowed by their Creator with certain unalienable rights, that among these are life, liberty and the pursuit of happiness." They put their lives on the line for the United States of America, and for the star-spangled banner, which yet waves "o'er the land of the free," and the what? "and the home of the brave." And after their last battle had been fought at Riva del Garda—they came home—home to you, for whom they had been fighting.

Spiritually, home is an important theme in the Bible. One way of understanding its message is to say that it's about finding home. It begins with Adam and Eve at first making their home in the Garden of Eden, and then because of sin losing their home; and it ends with God's people making their eternal home in the New Jerusalem. John Milton's *Paradise Lost* is about Adam and Eve's loss of their home in the Garden of Eden, and John Bunyan's *Pilgrim's Progress* is about a Christian's journey from his old home, the City of Destruction, to his new home in the Celestial City.

When Adam and Eve sinned, they were driven out of their home, the Garden of Eden, where God himself walked with them. For the rest of their 900+-year-long lives, they were exiles and wanderers in a land that went from being benevolent, to hostile. But sadly, they weren't the only ones exiled from their home that day, because we were exiled with them as well. We may never have been in the Garden of Eden, but intuitively we are aware that something very precious has been lost. Deep down we are aware that we were born into exile and that we, too, live in a hostile world. And I believe that every choice we make in this life—for good and for ill—is an effort to find our way home; to find our way to that place of ultimate security, rest and belonging that will never fail and will never pass away—and that we all long for.

In the passage I read a few moments ago, the author of the epistle to the Hebrews tells us that "By faith Abraham, when called to go to a place he would later receive as his inheritance, obeyed and went, even though he did not know where he was going." God had promised him a land that he and his descendants could call home, but, we read, "he made his home in the promised land like a stranger in a foreign country." In other words, Abraham lived in Canaan as a resident alien, not owning a square foot of ground, until the day he bought the field of Machpelah the Hittite as a burial site, when his wife, Sarah, died. And the author of Hebrews goes on to say that during all those long years Abraham was looking for a better inheritance; he was looking for an unseen city with real, eternal foundations—a city designed and built by God himself. And when Abraham, Isaac and Jacob all died, they still hadn't received what God had promised them. Rather, they acknowledged that they were strangers and exiles on the earth, and that they were still seeking a homeland, one that would be a better country—a city which God himself had prepared for them.

Adam and Eve, and Abraham could not go back to the Garden of Eden; and you and I cannot go back to Eden, either. Many have tried. Years ago, Di and I visited the Fruitlands Museum in Harvard, Massachusetts. There in 1843 Amos Bronson Alcott, the father of the novelist and poet Louisa May Alcott, started a utopian community called Fruitlands. The stated goal of the community was to "regain access to Eden." It lasted all of six months. And all such attempts to regain access to Eden are doomed to failure.

But while we cannot go back to Eden, we can move forward; we can find the security, the love and that sense of belongingness that home represents. God in his goodness has provided a means for us to find our way home. But for us *at the present time*, that home is not a *where*, it is a *who*; it is not a *place*, it is a *person*—it is the person of Jesus Christ. In John 14—hours before his betrayal, trial and death—Jesus says to his disciples "I will not leave you as orphans; I will come to you." And a few verses later he adds, "Anyone who loves me will obey my teaching. My Father will love him, and we will come to him and make our home with him."

And so, when we put our faith in Jesus Christ, he and his Father make their home with us; when we love Christ and obey his teaching, we find that we are loved by none-other than God himself; when we commit ourselves to him we find that rest for our weary souls for which we have been searching, even as we live in this world as exiles, aliens, and strangers.

Yet the day is coming when the *where* and the *who*, the *person* and the *place* will join together and will be one. Those looking to Christ await the fulfillment of Jesus' promise in John 14:2 and 3 that, "There are many rooms in my Father's House…And while it is true that I am going away to prepare a place for you, it is also true that I am coming again to welcome you into my own…home." And they await the literal fulfillment of Jesus' promise in Revelation 21, where we read, "Then I saw a new heaven and a new earth,…And I heard a loud voice from the throne saying, 'Behold! God's home is now among mankind, and he will make his home with them. They will be his people, and God himself will be with them and be their God. He will wipe every tear from their eyes, and there will be no more death or mourning or crying or pain, for the old order of things has died.'"

Your husbands, fathers, and grandfathers, and the other men of the 10th Mountain Division returned home from Europe in 1945 in triumph, and to much rejoicing—and rightly so. We owed them a debt of gratitude greater than we could repay. But take that triumph, and that rejoicing, and multiply it by a thousand—by a million. So shall it be when Jesus Christ returns at the end of the age to restore the Earth. He will set it free from every trace of sin, and every hint of suffering and sorrow; he will set it free from death; and there he will make his eternal home with his resurrected people. May that day come soon.

Are you restless this morning? You're homesick. Do you feel like a wanderer, but don't know why? You're homesick. Have you been searching for security, for a sense of belonging, for a place where you are both known and loved, but without success? You're homesick. Come to Jesus Christ this morning, and make him your home.

Advance comments on Bernie Marvin's *The Best of Bernie's Beat, Volume 2*

The first time we saw Bernie, he was in his Marine Corps dress blue uniform with the midnight blue coat with the seven gilt buttons, ribbons and medals, scarlet piped Mandarin collar, and the white web belt. He was in the church's parking lot organizing the host of participants who had arrived for Piermont's Memorial Day parade. To be honest, just the sight of him in that most handsome of all uniforms, was enough to intimidate us.

It was only a few years later, when he noticed Diane's "*I Love My Marine*" T-shirt, bought when our son completed his 13 weeks of recruit training, that we finally met Bernie. Since that day 11 years ago, he has become a good and trusted friend. He is an astute observer of and commentator on life, and the first article we turn to when the *Bridge Weekly* arrives is *Bernie's Beat.*

We may not read anything else in any given issue, but we always read his column. Whether Bernie is writing stories about local or national politics, Upper Valley goings-on, noteworthy people that he has met, military life or life in the Marvin family over the years (anyone want to learn how to bake bread?), it's always an instructive, informative and interesting read.

—**Mal Kircher**, Pastor, Piermont Congregational Church, Piermont, New Hampshire

---

In the second volume of *Bernie's Beat,* Marine veteran Bernie Marvin compiles stories of former service men and women who now call the Upper Valley home. Each of the 41 bite-sized chapters tells about the challenges these brave people faced in various wars. *The Best of Bernie's Beat, Volume 2* includes several of Bernie's own recollections, when as a young Marine he was shipped to Beirut, Lebanon, for combat duty. As if this mission as a Rifleman were not demanding enough, Bernie was also assigned to serve as a *Leatherneck Magazine* combat photographer.

Marvin's voice thrills his readers, making them feel as if they, too, are a part of the action—that they, too, went on the Bataan Death March with Bill White, were next to him on the dangerous boat trip to Japan and shared his enslavement as a coal miner and prisoner of war during World War II.

At times heartwarming, at times harrowing, these tales of courage and comradery are told in vivid detail. This book will delight not only military aficionados but also lovers of history and storytelling.

—**Polly H. Tafrate**, Piermont, New Hampshire and South Salem, New York

---

Ah, Bernie. We met the very first time when we started grade school classes at Wyman School in Winchester, Massachusetts.

All through the last few years in high school he became more and more interested in photography. I watched with envy his increasing skill with the Speed Graphic and remember him covering the Tech Tourney for *The Winchester Star* weekly newspaper.

Bernie's years as a combat photographer with the Marines allowed him to travel to far-off places and meet some of the great talent of the photography world. Through the years we have kept in touch and I wish we lived closer.

I truly admire Bernie's "Tom Clancy" method of approaching the local stories he writes, all the details that make the tale real and interesting.

Semper Fi!

— **Captain Pete Gamage**, US Air Force

Also by Bernie Marvin

The Best of *Bernie's Beat*: Volume 1
Stories of extraordinary people in New Hampshire's North Country
seen through the eyes of a veteran journalist

Made in the USA
Middletown, DE
24 November 2021